The Blessing

Gary Smalley & John Trent, Ph.D.

THOMAS NELSON PUBLISHERS
Nashville • Camden • Kansas City

Published in Nashville, Tennessee, by Thomas Nelson, Inc. and distributed in Canada by Lawson Falle, Ltd., Cambridge, Ontario.

Printed in the United States of America.

Unless otherwise noted all Scripture quotations are from THE NEW KING JAMES VERSION. Copyright © 1979, 1980, 1982, Thomas Nelson, Inc., Publishers.

Scripture quotations noted NIV are from The Holy Bible: New International Version. Copyright © 1978 by the New York International Bible Society. Used by permission of Zondervan Bible Publishers.

Scripture quotations noted KJV are from the King James Version of the Bible.

Scripture quotations noted NASB are from the New American Standard Bible, © The Lockman Foundation 1960, 1962, 1963, 1968, 1971, 1972, 1973, 1975, 1977, and are used by permission.

Names have been changed to protect the identities of people referred to in this book.

Library of Congress Cataloging-in-Publication Data

Smalley, Gary.
    The blessing.

    1. Family—Religious life.   2. Parenting—Religious aspects—Christianity.   3. Blessing and cursing.   4. Self-respect—Religious aspects—Christianity.
I. Trent, John T.   II. Title.
BV4526.2.S52   1986   249   86-5151
ISBN 0-8407-3066-7

5 6 7 8 9 10 11 - 97 96 95 94 93 92 91 90 89 88 87

Dedication

This book is dedicated to our wives, Norma and Cynthia, for their loving support and encouragement, and to four couples who have been a tremendous source of blessing to us in making this book possible: David and Karen Cavan, Doug and Judie Childress, Jerry and Judy LaBrasca, and Steve and Barbara Uhlman.

Contents

Acknowledgments

We would like to express our deepest thanks to the following people:

To Diana Trent, for the hours she put into proofreading the manuscript;

To Larry Weeden and Bruce Nygren, our editors at Thomas Nelson, for their encouragement and expertise;

To our teammate in ministry, Terry Brown, for his careful reading of the manuscript and helpful suggestions;

To the many individuals and small groups who were willing to offer their comments and suggestions to help us refine the concepts found in the book, especially to the following people: Randy Vogel, Pat Dixon, Richard and Donna Alverson, Chuck and Jane Beuerlein, Rick and Denita Ryan, Don and Nancy Schlander, and Rick and Angie Wonder.

—1—

In Search of the Blessing

❧

All of us long to be accepted by others. While we may say out loud, "I don't care what other people think about me," on the inside we all yearn for intimacy and affection. This yearning is especially true in our relationship with our parents. Gaining or missing out on parental approval has a tremendous effect on us, even if it has been years since we have had any regular contact with them. In fact, what happens in our relationship with our parents can greatly affect all our present and future relationships. While this may sound like an exaggeration, our office has been filled with people struggling with this very issue, people just like Brian and Nancy.

The Crushing of Brian's Dream

"Please say that you love me, please!" Brian's words trailed off into tears as he leaned over the now still form of his father. It was late at night in a large metropolitan hospital. Only the cold, white walls and the humming of a heart monitor kept Brian company. His tears revealed a deep inner pain and sensitivity that had tormented him for years, emotional wounds that now seemed beyond repair.

Brian had flown nearly halfway across the country to be at his father's side in one last attempt to try to reconcile years of misunderstanding and resentment. For years Brian had been searching for his father's acceptance and approval, but they always seemed just out of reach.

Brian's father had been a career Marine officer. His sole desire for Brian when he grew up was that he would follow in his father's footsteps. With that in mind, Brian's father took every opportunity to instill in his son discipline and the backbone he would need when one day he too was an officer.

Words of love or tenderness were forbidden. It was almost as if any slip into a display of warmth might crack the tough exterior Brian's father was trying to create in his son.

Brian was driven by his father to participate in sports and to take elective classes that would best equip him to be an officer. Brian's only praise for scoring a touchdown or doing well in a class was a lecture on how he could and should have done even better.

After graduating from high school, Brian did enlist in the Marine Corps. It was the happiest day of his father's life. However, his joy was short-lived. Cited for attitude problems and a disrespect for orders, his son was soon on report. After weeks of such reports (which included getting into a vicious fight with his drill instructor), Brian was dishonorably discharged from the service as incorrigible.

The news of Brian's dismissal from the Marines dealt a death blow to his relationship with his father. He was no longer welcome in his father's home, and for years there was no contact between them.

During those years, Brian struggled with feelings of inferiority and lacked self-confidence. Even though he was above average in intelligence, he worked at various jobs far below his abilities. Three times he had been engaged—only to break the engagement just weeks before the wedding. Somehow he just didn't believe that another person could really love him.

Although Brian was unaware of it at the time, he was

experiencing common symptoms of growing up without a sense of the family blessing, a missing element in his life that finally led him to seek professional help.

We began counseling with Brian after he had broken his second engagement. As he peeled away the layers of his past, Brian began to see both his need for his family's blessing and his responsibility for dealing honestly with his parents. That is when the call came from his mother saying that his father was dying from a heart attack.

Brian went immediately to the hospital to see his father. The entire flight he was filled with hope that now, at long last, they could talk and reconcile their relationship. "I'm sure he'll listen to me. I've learned *so* much. I know things are going to change between us." Brian repeated these phrases over and over to himself during the flight. But it was not to be.

Brian's father slipped into a coma a few hours before he arrived. The words that Brian longed to hear for the first time—words of love and acceptance—now could never be spoken. Four hours after Brian arrived at the hospital, his father died without regaining consciousness.

"Dad, please wake up!" Brian's heartbreaking sobs echoed down the hospital corridor. His cries spoke of an incredible sense of loss: not only the physical loss of his father, but, like many others, also the emotional sense of losing any chance of his father's blessing.

Nancy Relives a Painful Past

Nancy's loss was a different sort, but the hurt and pain she received from missing out on the blessing stung her just as deeply. In fact, living apart from the blessing had caused problems not only with her parents, but with her husband and children as well.

Nancy grew up in an affluent suburb outside a major city. During Nancy's early years, her mother loved to socialize with other women at the club and at frequent civic activities. In fact, with a marriage that was less than fulfilling, these social gatherings became of paramount importance to Nancy's mother.

When Nancy was very young, her mother would dress her up in elegant clothes (the kind you had to sit still in, not play in) and take her and her older sister to the club. But as Nancy grew older, this practice began to change.

Unlike her mother and older sister, Nancy was not petite. In fact, she was quite large and big-boned. Neither was Nancy a model of tranquility. She was a tomboy who loved outdoor games, swinging on fences, and animals of all kinds.

As you might imagine, such behavior from a daughter who was being groomed to be a debutante caused real problems—especially when a garter snake mysteriously found its way into one of her mother's outdoor teas. No one could prove that Nancy had let the snake into the garden, but from that moment on, things began to change in her relationship with her mother.

Nancy's mother tried desperately to mend her daughter's erring ways. Nancy was constantly scolded about being "awkward" and "clumsy." During shopping sprees, Nancy was often subjected to verbal barbs designed to motivate her to lose weight. "All the really nice clothes are two sizes too small for you. They're your *sister's* size," her mother would taunt. Nancy was finally forced on a strict diet to try to make her physically presentable to others.

Nancy tried hard to stick to her diet and be all her mother wanted. However, more and more often Nancy's mother and sister would go to social events and leave Nancy at home. Soon all invitations to join these functions stopped. After all, her mother told her, "You don't want to be embarrassed because of the way you look with all the other children around, do you?"

When Nancy first came in for counseling, she was in her thirties, married, and the mother of two children. For years she had struggled with her weight and with feelings of inferiority. Her marriage had been a constant struggle for her as well.

Nancy's husband loved her and was deeply committed to her, but her inability to feel acceptable left her constantly insecure and defensive. As a result of this hypersensitivity, every time she and her husband began to draw close, Nancy would feel threatened. Invariably, some small thing her husband did would set her off, and her marriage was back at arm's length.

Frankly, because of her lack of acceptance in the past, being at arm's length was the only place Nancy felt comfortable in a relationship. Her marriage was certainly of concern to her. Yet where Nancy struggled most was with her children, and with one child in particular.

Nancy had two daughters. The older girl was big-boned and looked very much like Nancy, but the younger daughter was a beautiful, petite child. What was causing Nancy incredible pain was the relationship between her mother and this younger child and the effect of that relationship on Nancy's feelings and behavior.

Just like in Nancy's childhood, her mother catered to the younger "pretty" daughter, while the older daughter was left out and ignored. Old hurts and wounds that Nancy thought were hidden in her past were now being relived through watching her own children. The heartache and loneliness that her older daughter was feeling was an echo of Nancy's unhappiness.

In spite of herself, Nancy's attitude toward her younger daughter began to change. The slightest annoying thing this child did brought an explosion of anger. Bitterness and resentment began to replace genuine affection.

In her heart of hearts, Nancy was also angry at God. In spite of her prayers, she felt He had changed neither her relationship with her mother nor her present circumstances. She seemed doomed to repeat vicariously through her daughters her own painful past. As a result of this barrage of feelings, she stopped going to her Bible study group, calling Christian friends, and even praying to God.

For Nancy, her relationship with her husband, her children, and God had all been affected by missing out on the blessing that she had tried for years to grasp, but that never quite came within reach.

Our Need for Acceptance

For Brian and for Nancy, the absence of parental acceptance had serious consequences. For Brian, the lack of the blessing was a major reason for his broken engagements and for keeping him from getting close enough to another person to become genuinely committed. For Nancy, an inability to feel acceptable as a person was destroying her most important relationships. Without realizing it, Brian and Nancy were searching for the same thing—their family's blessing.

Brian and Nancy typify people who are searching for their family's blessing. For years after they had moved away from home *physically,* they still remained chained to the past *emotionally.* Their lack of approval from their parents in the past kept a feeling of genuine acceptance from others in the present from taking root in their lives. In Nancy's case, this lack of approval even kept her from believing that her heavenly Father truly accepted her.

Some people are driven toward workaholism as they search for the blessing they never received at home. Always striving for acceptance, they never feel satisfied that they are measuring up. Others get mired in withdrawal and apathy as they give up hope of ever truly being blessed. Unfortunately, this withdrawal can become so severe that it can lead to chronic depression and even suicide. For almost all children who miss out on their parents' blessing, at some level this lack of acceptance sets off a lifelong search.

This search for the blessing is not just a modern-day phenomenon. It is actually centuries old. In fact, we can find a graphic picture in the Old Testament of a person who missed out on his family's blessing. This person was a confused and angry man named Esau. As we look at this man's life, we will also begin to learn about the blessing and what it can mean to grow up with or without it.

"Bless Me, Even Me Also, O My Father!"

Esau was beside himself. *Could this really be happening?* he may have thought. Perhaps his mind went back to the events of that day. Just hours before, his father had called him to his side and made a special request. If Esau, the older son, would go and bring in fresh game for a savory meal, his father's long-awaited blessing would be given to him.

What was this blessing that Esau had waited for over the years? For sons or daughters in biblical times, receiving their father's blessing was a momentous event. We will discover that it gave these children a tremendous sense of being highly valued by their parents and even pictured a special future for them. At a specific point in their lives they would hear words of encouragement, love, and acceptance from their parents.

We will see that some aspects of this Old Testament blessing were unique to that time. However, the *relationship elements* of this blessing are still applicable today. In Old Testament times, this blessing was primarily reserved for one special occasion. In contrast, parents today can decide to build these elements of blessing into their children's lives daily.

For Esau, his father, Isaac, followed the custom of waiting until a specific day to give his son the blessing. Now at long last, Esau's waiting was over. His time of blessing would begin as soon as he could catch and prepare a special meal.

With all the skill and abilities of an experienced hunter, Esau had quickly and efficiently gone about his work. In almost no time a delicious stew was prepared as only one familiar with the art of cooking in the field could do.

All had been done just as he was told. Why, then, had

his father trembled so when Esau stood before him? As if
in a dream, the scene played over and over in Esau's
mind. He had just entered his father's tent and greeted
him:

> "Let my father arise and eat of his son's game, that your
> soul may bless me." And his father Isaac said to him,
> "Who are you?" And he said, "I am your son, your first-
> born, Esau."
>
> Then Isaac trembled exceedingly, and said, "Who? Where
> is the one who hunted game and brought it to me? I ate all
> of it before you came, and I have blessed him—and indeed
> he shall be blessed."
>
> When Esau heard the words of his father, he cried with an
> exceedingly great and bitter cry, and said to his father,
> *"Bless me, even me also, O my father!"* (Gen. 27:31–34,
> italics added).

Little did Esau know that when his aged and nearly
blind father had called him to his side, another had been
listening. Rebekah, the mother of Esau and his twin
brother, Jacob, was also in the tent. As soon as Esau went
out into the fields to hunt fresh game, she ran to her favorite son, Jacob, with a cunning plan.

If they hurried, they could kill a young kid from the
flock and prepare a savory meal. What's more, they
could dress Jacob in his brother's clothing and put animal skins on him to simulate Esau's rough and hairy
arms, hands, and neck.

Putting on Esau's clothes did not present a problem,
but one thing they couldn't counterfeit was Esau's voice.
That almost blew the whistle on them (Gen. 27:22). But
even though Isaac was a little skeptical, ultimately their
plan worked just as they had hoped it would. We read in
Genesis 27:22–23, "So Jacob went near to Isaac his
father. . . . And he did not recognize him, because his
hands were hairy like his brother Esau's hands; so he
blessed him." The blessing meant for the older son went
to the younger.

Years before, Esau had sold his birthright to his
brother, Jacob, for only a bowl of soup (Gen. 25:29–34).

As we will see later, this birthright was a special right to the inheritance that was reserved for the firstborn. Esau was willing to trade that away without a second thought to meet a momentary hunger pang, but losing the family blessing was another story.

When Esau lost his blessing from his father, he was devastated. In fact, when he discovered that Jacob had stolen the blessing, Esau cried out, "Do you have only *one* blessing, my father? Bless me, even me also, O my father!" (Gen. 27:38). For a father in biblical times, once a blessing was spoken, it was irretrievable. In response to his pitiful cries, Esau did receive a blessing of sorts from his father (Gen. 27:39–40), but it was not the words of value and acceptance that he had longed to hear.

Can you feel the anguish in the cry, "Bless me, even me also, O my father"? This same painful cry and unfulfilled longing is being echoed today by many people who are searching for their family's blessing, men and women whose parents, for whatever reason, have failed to bless them with words of love and acceptance. People just like Brian and Nancy. People you rub shoulders with every day. Perhaps even you.

The Importance of the Blessing Today

Genuine acceptance; an unmet need in Brian, Nancy, and Esau's lives; a need that goes unmet in thousands of lives today—perhaps you have this need or a loved one is struggling with it, a need that the blessing helps to meet. Yet, the family blessing not only provides people a much needed sense of personal acceptance, it also plays an important part in protecting and even freeing them to develop intimate relationships.

Today, as in centuries past, orthodox Jewish homes bestow a special family blessing on their children. This blessing is much like the patriarchal blessing we were introduced to in the story of Esau. This blessing has been an important part of providing a sense of acceptance for generations of children. But recently, it has also provided an important source of protection to those children.

All across the country, cults are holding out a counterfeit blessing to our children. Cult leaders have mastered the elements of the blessing we will describe in the pages that follow. Providing a sense of family and holding out (at least initially) the promise of personal attention, affection, and affirmation is an important drawing card for many of these cults. Children who grow up without a sense of parental acceptance are especially susceptible to being drawn in. In fact, thousands are every year. However, like beckoning hungry children to an imaginary dinner, the smell and aroma may draw them to the table; but after eating they are left hungrier than before.

If you are a parent, learning about the family blessing can help you provide your child or children with a protective tool. The best defense against a child's longing for imaginary acceptance is to provide him or her with genuine acceptance. By providing a child with genuine acceptance and affirmation at home, you can greatly reduce the likelihood that he or she will seek acceptance in the arms of a cult member or with someone in an immoral relationship. Genuine acceptance radiates from the concept of the blessing.

However, the blessing is not just an important tool for parents to use. The blessing is also of critical importance for anyone who desires to cleave, or draw close, to another person in an intimate relationship.

One of the most familiar verses in the Bible is Genesis 2:24: "For this cause a man shall leave his father and his mother, and shall cleave to his wife" (NASB). Many books and tapes talk about the need to cleave to our spouse. However, very few talk about the tremendous need people have to "leave" home. Perhaps this is because people have often thought of leaving home as simply moving away physically.

In reality, leaving home has always meant much more than putting physical distance between our parents and ourselves. In the Old Testament, for example, the farthest most people would actually move away from their parents was across the campfire and into another tent! Leaving home carries with it not only the idea of physical separation but also of *emotional* separation as well.[1]

The terrible fact is that most people who have missed out on their parents' blessing have great emotional difficulty leaving home. It may have been years since they have seen their parents, but unmet needs for personal acceptance can keep a person emotionally chained to his or her parents' home, unable to genuinely cleave to another person in a lasting relationship. For this reason many couples never get off the ground in terms of marital intimacy. This is what happened to Brian and Nancy. You or a loved one may be facing this problem. Understanding the concept of the blessing is crucial to defeating the problem and freeing people to build healthy relationships.

A Journey of Hope and Healing

In a world awash with insecurity and in search of acceptance, we need biblical anchors to hold on to. The search for acceptance that Brian and Nancy and so many others go through often leads people to accept a cure that is worse than the problem itself. Finding oneself through traumatic re-creations of the past or losing oneself through hypnosis or a similar psychological technique seldom, if ever, offers lasting change. On the other hand, God's Word and His principles do offer a changeless blueprint for constructing or reconstructing relationships.

In the pages that follow, you will discover more about the blessing. If you are a parent, you will see how to give your children the blessing and how to discern if they have it now. You can also evaluate whether your parents received the blessing and how that may have affected their attitudes toward you. For those of you who grew up with the blessing, you will see how your parents communicated it and will be encouraged to express your thanks to them.

We also offer help if you had to grow up without your parents' blessing. You will gain insight into common patterns of those who grow up without the blessing. You can discover practical lessons on living apart from an earthly family blessing. And you will be exposed to God's spiritual family blessing that is offered to each of His children. There is hope for ending the search for personal acceptance you may have been on for years.

If you are a teacher, discovering the blessing can help you better understand your students. If you counsel others, it can provide a helpful framework for understanding many problems and offering practical solutions. If you are involved in ministering to others, it can help you understand a crucial need every person has and give you resources to meet that need.

Our prayer is that in the pages that follow, you will take the time and have the courage to journey into the past, a journey that can lead to hope and healing. Even more, we pray that you will be willing to look honestly at the present and apply the things you will discover.

These pages may end a lifelong search for you or begin a new relationship with your children, your spouse, your parents, or a close friend. Our deepest desire is that this book will enrich your relationship with your heavenly Father as you learn more about the source of blessing He is to each believer. All this as we look at the family blessing—yesterday and today.

—2—

The Blessing: Yesterday and Today

─────────────── ⊷ ───────────────

*J*ust what is this blessing that seems to be so important? Does it really apply to us today, or was it just something for Old Testament times? What are the elements of which it consists? How can I know whether I have received it or whether my children are experiencing it now?

These questions commonly surface when we introduce people to the blessing. In answering them, we will discover five powerful relationship elements that the Old Testament blessing contains. The presence or absence of these elements can help us determine whether our home is, or our parents' home was, a place of blessing. In this chapter, we will also look at how orthodox Jewish homes have bestowed a blessing on their children and why they have done so down through the centuries.

A study of the blessing always begins in the context of parental acceptance. However, in studying the blessing in the Scriptures, we found that its principles can be used in any intimate relationship.

Husbands can apply these principles in blessing their wives, and wives their husbands. Friendships can be deepened and strengthened by including each element of the blessing. These key ingredients when applied in a church family can bring warmth, healing, and hope to

our brothers and sisters in Christ, many who never received an earthly blessing from their parents. As we will
see in a later chapter, they are the very relationship elements God uses in blessing His children.

Is the blessing we build into a person's life today exactly like the blessing in the Old Testament? Certainly
not. While the basic relationship elements of blessing remain the same, the Scriptures contain several spiritual
aspects of the blessing that were unique to that time.

Unique Aspects of the Blessing in the Old Testament

One way we can see the unique spiritual side of the
family blessing is to look at how God used this concept to
identify His line of blessing through one family until the
coming of Christ.

God's covenant of blessing was originally made with
and was to pass directly through one family's offspring.[1]
Abraham's descendants received the blessing God had
promised them (Gen. 12:2–3). This was true generation
after generation right up until the birth of the Messiah
(Matt. 1:2–16). In contrast, because of what Jesus did for
all people, now every family and each family member
can experience a blessing through God's Son. This blessing can then be passed on to others by introducing them
to Christ.

Another spiritual meaning associated with the blessing is how it pictures God's sovereign choice. With Jacob
and Esau and with another set of brothers, Ephraim and
Manasseh, God's sovereignty was pictured in who first
received their family's blessing and who did not (Gen.
49:14; Rom. 9:11–13). As we will see later in this chapter,
the Old Testament blessing also had a prophetic aspect
that does not apply to parents today.

However, in addition to the unique spiritual meanings
attached to the family blessing, the blessing always has
had an intensely personal side to it as well. This deeply

personal meaning can be seen in the heart-wrenching cries Esau uttered when he lost his father's blessing. He was not crying over the loss of an objective theological concept, but over the deeply personal words from his father that eluded him.

The personal, or relational, side of using the blessing to communicate parental love and acceptance is what orthodox Jewish homes have continued to practice in blessing children. While they recognized the unique spiritual and prophetic aspects of the blessing the patriarchs gave their children, they adopted the basic relationship elements of the blessing laid down in the Scriptures to encourage their children. These tools communicate acceptance and affirmation and still apply to men and women today.

The Basic Elements of the Blessing

What are these elements, and how do they work together? While neither of the authors admits to being an expert gardener, an elementary understanding of how a flower grows can help us picture the way the basic components of the blessing work together.

A flower cannot grow unless it has the necessary elements of life. Every flower needs soil, air, water, light, and a secure place to grow (one where its roots are not constantly being pulled out). When these five basic ingredients are present, it is almost impossible to keep a flower from growing. The same thing is true when it comes to the basic elements of the blessing.

Like the basic needs a flower has, the blessing also has five key elements. These five elements, blended together, can cause personal acceptance to blossom and grow in our home today. Each individual part provides a unique contribution. Each is needed in giving the blessing.

In later chapters, we will look in detail at each of these five elements. But for now, we will introduce them briefly.

A definition of the family blessing that contains its five major elements reads:

A family blessing begins with *meaningful touching*. It continues with a *spoken message* of *high value*, a message that pictures a *special future* for the individual being blessed, and one that is based on an *active commitment* to see the blessing come to pass.

Here is another way to look at the five basic parts of the blessing:

The family blessing includes:
- Meaningful Touch
- A Spoken Message
- Attaching "High Value" to the One Being Blessed
- Picturing a Special Future for the One Being Blessed
- An Active Commitment to Fulfill the Blessing

Let's look a little closer at each of these.

MEANINGFUL TOUCH

Meaningful touch was an essential element in bestowing the blessing in Old Testament homes. So it was with Isaac when he went to bless his son. We read in Genesis 27:26 that Isaac said, "Come near now and kiss me, my son." This incident was not an isolated one. Each time the blessing was given in the Scriptures, meaningful touching provided a caring background to the words that would be spoken. Kissing, hugging, or the laying on of hands were all a part of bestowing the blessing.

Meaningful touching has many beneficial effects. As we will see in the next chapter, the act of touch is a key to communicating warmth, personal acceptance, affirmation—even physical health! For Isaac, as well as for any person who wishes to see the blessing grow and develop in a child, spouse, or friend, touch is an integral part of the blessing.

A SPOKEN MESSAGE

The second element of our definition is based on a spoken message. In many homes today, words of love and acceptance are seldom heard. A tragic misconception parents in these homes share is that simply being present communicates the blessing. Nothing could be further from the truth. A blessing becomes so only when it is spoken.

For a child in search of the blessing, the major thing silence communicates is confusion. Children who are left to fill in the blanks when it comes to what their parents think about them will often fail the test when it comes to feeling valuable and secure. Spoken words at least give the hearer an indication that he or she is worthy of some attention. I (John) learned this lesson on the football field.

When I began playing football in high school, one particular coach thought I was filled with raw talent (emphasis on the "raw"!). He was constantly chewing me out. And he even took extra time after practice to point out mistakes I was making. After I missed an important block in practice one day (a frequent occurrence), this coach stood right in my face and chewed me out six ways to Sunday.

When he finally finished, he had me go over to the sidelines with the other players who were not a part of the scrimmage. Standing next to me was a third-string player who rarely got into the game. I can remember leaning over to him and saying, "Boy, I wish he would get off my case." "Don't say that," my teammate replied. "At least he's talking to you. If he ever *stops* talking to you, that means he's given up on you."

Many adults we see in counseling interpret their parents' silence in exactly the same way. They feel as though they are "third-string" children to their parents. Their parents may have provided a roof over their heads (or even a Porsche to drive), but without spoken words of blessing, they are left unsure of their personal worth and acceptance.

Abraham spoke his blessing to his son Isaac. Isaac spoke a blessing to his son Jacob. Jacob gave a verbal blessing to each of his twelve sons and to two of his grandchildren. When God blessed us with the gift of His Son, it was His *Word* that "became flesh and dwelt among us" (John 1:14). God has always been a God of the spoken word.

"But I don't yell at my children or cut them down like some parents," some may say. Unfortunately, even a lack of negative words does not translate into a spoken blessing. We will see this lack illustrated in several painful examples in a later chapter.

To see the blessing bloom and grow in the life of a child, spouse, or friend, we need to verbalize our message. Good intentions aside, good *words* are necessary to provide genuine acceptance.

ATTACHING HIGH VALUE

Meaningful touch and a spoken message: These first two elements lead up to the words of blessing themselves, words of high value.

To value something means to attach honor to it. In fact, this is the meaning of the verb "to bless." In Hebrew, the word *bless* literally means "to bow the knee."[2] This word was used in showing reverence, even awe, to an important person. Now, this doesn't mean that in order to bless a person we are to stand back, fall to our knees, and bow before that person in awe! Nonetheless, words of blessing should carry with them the recognition that this person is valuable and has redeeming qualities. In the Scriptures, recognition is based on who they are, not simply on their performance.

In blessing his son, Isaac says, "Surely, the smell of my son / Is like the smell of a field / Which the LORD has blessed. . . .Let peoples serve you, / And nations bow down to you" (Gen. 27:27–29). That pictures a very valuable person! Not just anybody merits having nations bow down to him!

As you may have noticed, Isaac uses a word picture to describe how valuable his son is to him. ("The smell of my son is like the smell of a field which the LORD has blessed.") Word pictures are a powerful way of communicating acceptance. Later, we will look not only at the use of these word pictures, but we will also learn how to use them in giving a blessing. In the Old Testament, they were a key to communicating to a child, a spouse, or a friend a message of high value—the third element of the family blessing.

PICTURING A SPECIAL FUTURE

A fourth element of the blessing is the way it pictures a special future for the person being blessed. Isaac says to his son Jacob, "May God give you / Of the dew of heaven, / Of the fatness of the earth. . . . Let peoples serve you, / And nations bow down to you" (Gen. 27:28–29). Even today, Jewish homes are noted for picturing a special future for their children. One story we heard illustrates this activity very well.

Sidel, a young Jewish mother, was proudly walking down the street pushing a stroller with her infant twins. As she rounded the corner, she saw her neighbor, Sarah. "My, what beautiful children," Sarah cooed. "What are their names?" Pointing to each child, Sidel replied, "This is Bennie, the doctor, and Reuben, the lawyer." This woman believed her children had a special future and great potential before them! Isaac believed that about his son, and we should communicate this message to those we seek to bless.

One distinction should be made between Isaac's blessing and picturing a special future for a person today. Because of Isaac's unique position as a patriarch (God's appointed leader and a father of the nation of Israel), his words to Jacob carried with them the weight of biblical prophecy. This position was also true of Jacob later in the book of Genesis. His blessing to each of his sons pictured their future exactly as it would unfold for them.

As parents or loved ones today, we cannot predict another person's future with biblical accuracy. We can, however, encourage and help them to set meaningful goals. We can also convey to them that the gifts and character traits they have right now are attributes that God can bless and use in the future.

Psychological visualization and picturing grandiose accomplishments in the future will not give a person the blessing. If anything, such practices pile up unattainable expectations that can move the person further away from genuine acceptance.[3] However, as we will see in a later chapter, our Lord Himself speaks quite often about our future. In fact, He goes to great lengths to assure us of our present relationship with Him and of the ocean full of blessings in store for us as His children in the future.

As we will see in a later chapter, we can use a healthy, biblical way to picture a special future for our children. With this fourth element of the blessing, a child can gain a sense of security in the present and grow in confidence to serve God and others in the future.

AN ACTIVE COMMITMENT

The last element of the blessing pictures the *responsibility* that goes with giving the blessing. For the patriarchs, not only their words, but God Himself stood behind the blessing they bestowed on their children. Several times, God spoke directly through the angel of the Lord to the patriarchs confirming His active commitment to their family line.

Parents today, in particular, need to rely on the Lord to give them the strength and staying power to confirm their children's blessing. They too have God's Word through the Scriptures as a guide, plus the power of the indwelling Holy Spirit.

Why is active commitment so important when it

comes to bestowing the blessing? Words alone cannot communicate the blessing; they need to be backed with a commitment to do everything possible to help the one blessed be successful. We can tell a child, "You have the talent to be a very good pianist." But, if we neglect to provide a piano for that child to practice on, our lack of commitment has undermined our message.

When it comes to spending time with our children or helping them develop a certain skill, some children hear, "Wait until the weekend." Then it becomes "wait until *another* weekend" so many times that they no longer believe our commitments match our words.

Later we will look at a key to helping us stay actively committed to our children. It involves actually becoming a student of our children (or spouse or friend) in order to learn how we can genuinely bless them. This fifth element of the blessing, an active commitment, is crucial to seeing the blessing communicated in our homes.

Provide a flower with the essential elements it needs, and watch it grow! Provide the five basic ingredients of the blessing—meaningful touch, a spoken message, attaching high value to the one being blessed, picturing a special future for them, and confirming the blessing by an active commitment—and personal acceptance can thrive and bloom in a home.

To further understand the blessing in the Scriptures, let's turn our attention to the way it has been used in Jewish homes. For centuries, the blessing of children has been an important part of Jewish family life. In terms of communicating acceptance and affirmation, they have much to teach us about providing a blessing for important people in our lives.

The Blessing and Jewish Family Life

Before the children can walk, they should be carried on the Sabbath and on the Holy Days to their father and mother to receive their blessing.

After they are able to walk, they should go to them of

their own accord, with body bent and with head bowed, to receive the Blessing.

(From the *Brantshpiegal*, a book on Jewish family life and practices written in 1602.)

From Old Testament times to today, the blessing has been an important gift offered to Jewish children. In fact, it has been a *duty* of parents to their children.[4] It has also been a regular part of the rabbis' duties toward children on *Shabat* (the Sabbath) and on feast and holy days.[5]

The earliest Jewish families we see are, of course, recorded in the Scriptures. The practice of blessing children was probably familiar to Abraham, even before God called him out from Ur of the Chaldees. All across Egypt and the Middle East, the practice of giving a blessing to children was common.[6]

In Old Testament times, each child in the family was given a general blessing as well as a special blessing for the firstborn. Esau, whom we saw in the first chapter, looked forward to receiving his blessing as the firstborn son in his family. In Genesis 49, not only the oldest, but each of Jacob's twelve sons, received a blessing from their father. While there were additional *privileges* that went to the firstborn, the essential *elements* of both blessings were the same as those we listed above. What were some of the special additional privileges the firstborn child might enjoy?

Firstborn daughters had the right to be married before a younger sister. Laban observed this custom in arranging for Jacob to marry his oldest daughter, Leah. Only after she was married was Jacob allowed to marry Laban's younger daughter, Rachel (Gen. 29:21–30). (That certainly wasn't the way Jacob had planned it, by the way!) In addition, ancient tablets found in Syria spoke of special rights of inheritance that belonged to the firstborn daughter.[7]

Firstborn sons made out even better. For one thing, their blessing bequeathed to them *twice* the inheritance of any other brother (2 Kings 2:9). That was reason enough for Esau to be excited about receiving the blessing and for being upset when he lost it!

The firstborn son's blessing had other aspects. The firstborn son was designated as the leader of the family when the father died. It would become his responsibility to be the spiritual leader in the home. All in all, firstborn children received many special privileges.

An Old Testament law prohibited arbitrarily bypassing the eldest son to give the firstborn's blessing to another child (Deut. 21:15–17), but it certainly could happen and was done quite frequently. This even happened in Jacob's family. Reuben was the firstborn son of twelve brothers, but it was Joseph, the next to the youngest, who actually received the firstborn's blessing (Gen. 48:22). Many ancient tablets mentioned that the shifting of the blessing from one child to the other—whether sons or daughters—was quite common during this period.[8]

As we have seen in our look at Old Testament times, parents gave a *general blessing* to each child and sometimes reserved a *special blessing* for the firstborn. While the firstborn could receive certain privileges a younger child did not, the basic elements of both blessings remained the same.

The next stop in our look at how Jewish families adopted the blessing comes during New Testament times, the time of the Pharisees. During this period there were rules and regulations for nearly every event—the blessing of children not excluded. Around the time of Christ's birth, Rabbi Jesus ben Sirach wrote, "The blessing of the father builds houses for the sons; the blessing of the mother fills them with good things."[9]

While there remained a general blessing for children during this time, a definite trend to favor blessing sons instead of daughters developed. This tendency is seen in many of the Hebrew commentaries on the law that sprang up during that day.

In an explanation of the priestly benediction, "The

LORD bless thee and keep thee" (Num. 6:24), one rabbi wrote, "May the Lord bless thee with sons, and keep thee from daughters because they need careful guarding!"[10] In even stronger language, another rabbi wrote, "What is the interpretation of the words 'all things' in the Scripture, 'The Lord blessed Abraham in all things'? That he had no daughter!"[11] There was a lot of humor in those words—as long as you weren't a daughter.

While the tendency to bless only sons was present, exceptions to the rule were made in some Jewish homes with some religious leaders. In fact, another man some called rabbi during this same period welcomed both sons *and* daughters to receive His blessing. We read in Mark 10:13–16:

> Then they brought young children to Him, that He might touch them; but the disciples rebuked those who brought them. But when Jesus saw it, He was greatly displeased and said to them, "Let the little children come to Me, and do not forbid them. . . ." And He took them up in His arms, put His hands on them, and *blessed* them (Mark 10:13–16, italics added).

Jesus knew that both little boys *and* little girls needed the elements of the blessing.[12] In a later chapter, we will see that in almost every detail, His blessing of children parallels the important elements of the family blessing.

Looking to modern-day Jewish homes and practices, the blessing is still an important concept in many orthodox families. At many Shabat (Sabbath) services, the parents are to bring their children for a special blessing. There the rabbi will call the children in the congregation forward to receive their blessing. Acting on behalf of the parents, the rabbi will lay his hand on the head of each child and recite words like these, "May God bless you and make you as Ephraim and Manasseh."

This blessing originally comes from Genesis 48:20, where Jacob was blessing Joseph's two sons—Jacob's *grandchildren*. Listen to the blessing this aging patriarch bestows on these two young boys: "So he blessed them that day, saying, 'By you Israel will bless, saying, "May

God make you as Ephraim and as Manasseh!" ' " What a blessing! Even today, centuries later, in synagogues and in Jewish homes, this blessing is a favorite for parents to use with their children.

While studying how the blessing is given in modern Jewish homes, we had the privilege of speaking with several rabbis. In our interviews, we discovered that bestowing a family blessing was still very much alive. The family blessing is considered an important vehicle for communicating a sense of identity, meaning, love, and acceptance. In fact, in many orthodox homes, a weekly blessing is given by the father to each of his children. With the ceremonial candles lit, a time of blessing begins.

Sharing special meals; kissing, hugging, or the laying on of hands; creating a word picture or using one in the Scriptures to praise a child; even asking God to provide a special future for each child are common elements of blessing children in orthodox homes today.

While the blessing is an ancient practice, it still holds important keys to granting genuine acceptance. From a blessing to the firstborn to special words of love and acceptance for each child, the blessing remains a part of Jewish family life today. For Christian parents who have the hope and reality of Jesus, the Messiah, and His love, their blessing can be even more powerful.

At Home with the Family Blessing

We have looked at the basic elements of the blessing and at how it has been carried on for centuries in Jewish homes. Our aim now is to become very practical as we look closely at each of the five key elements of the blessing. Learning more about these powerful tools for communicating personal and parental approval can help us become a source of blessing to our children, spouse, brothers and sisters in Christ, and others.

Some of you who are reading this book may already feel a little discouraged. In reading about the key elements of the blessing, perhaps you realized for the first time that you never got the blessing from your parents, or that it is not an active part of your relationship with your children. Please don't lose heart. As we look closely at the five basic elements of the blessing, you can gain practical skills to become a source of blessing to others. Later, you will also discover how to deal effectively with missing out on the blessing in your life.

Together, we will stop in several of the most common homes we see in counseling that *withhold* the blessing from their children. And we will look at God's provision for dealing with the loss of an earthly family blessing. We will also look at several modern-day homes that are models for bestowing the blessing on children, spouse, church family, and friends.

With that in mind, let's turn our attention to the first element of the blessing, meaningful touch. Harnessed within this first key to communicating personal acceptance is an incredible power to bless, right at our fingertips.

—3—

The First Element of the Blessing:
Meaningful Touch

———————— ✌ ————————

A little four-year-old girl became frightened late one night during a thunderstorm. After one particularly loud clap of thunder, she jumped up from her bed, ran down the hall, and burst into her parents' room. Jumping right in the middle of the bed, she sought out her parents' arms for comfort and assurance. "Don't worry, Honey," her father said, trying to calm her fears. "The Lord will protect you." The little girl snuggled closer to her father and said, "I know that, Daddy, but right now I need someone with skin on!"

The honesty of some children! This little one did not doubt her heavenly Father's ability to protect her, but she was also aware that He had given her an earthly father she could run to: someone whom God had entrusted with a special gift that could bring her comfort, security, and personal acceptance—the blessing of meaningful touch.

This little girl was fortunate. Her father was willing to share this important aspect of the blessing with his daughter. Not all children are as fortunate. Even in caring homes, most parents (particularly fathers) will stop touching their children once the children reach the grade school years.[1] When they do stop touching them, an important part of giving their children the blessing stops as well.

For a four-year-old, being held and touched is permissible in most homes. But what about the need a fourteen-year-old has to be meaningfully touched by his mother or father? (Even if the teenager outwardly cringes every time he or she is hugged.) Or a thirty-four-year-old? Or your spouse or a close friend?

Your spouse and others need meaningful touch. However, children are particularly affected by touch deprivation. Sometimes the absence of touch can so affect a child that he or she spends a lifetime reaching out for arms that will never embrace him or her.

"I wish. . . . I wish. . . ." Lisa had slumped down in her chair, hugging herself and rocking backward and forward as she repeated these words. Lisa was a new adolescent patient in the psychiatric ward where I (John) was a seminary intern. Whenever she felt afraid or sad, she would wrap herself in her arms and rock back and forth.

We found that Lisa had behaved this way since she was seven years old. That was when her mother had abandoned her at an orphanage.

Lisa was trying to escape the hurt and pain she was feeling by holding herself. Lisa had no one else to hold her; all she had was the wish her mother would return. She needed meaningful touching so much that she would wrap her arms around *herself* and try to hug away the hurt.

The Blessing: Meaningful Touch

In the Scriptures, touch played an important part in the bestowal of the family blessing. When Isaac blessed Jacob, an embrace and a kiss were involved. We read, "Then his father Isaac said to him, 'Please come close and kiss me, my son'" (Gen. 27:26 NASB).

The Hebrew word for "come close" is very descriptive. It is used of armies drawn together in battle. It is even used to picture the overlapping scales on a crocodile's skin. [2] It may have been a while since you last saw a battle or a crocodile, but these word pictures still call up in our minds a picture of a very close connection.

Isaac wasn't asking his son to give him an "Aunt Ethel hug." (Remember Aunt Ethel—the one who pinched your cheek and then repeatedly patted you on the back when she hugged you like she was bringing up gas?) Free of the current taboos our culture sets on a man embracing his son, Isaac was calling Jacob close to give him a bear hug.

This hug is even more special because Jacob was not four, but at least forty years old; and he was still encouraged to give his dad a hug and a kiss.[3] As we have seen with Lisa and will see later, our need for meaningful touch does not go away when we enter grade school. Isaac modeled someone who didn't set up barriers around the need to be touched. He was a model that parents, husbands and wives, and even friends at church need to follow in giving the blessing.

In the Scriptures, we find another clear example of including meaningful touch in bestowing the blessing. This time the blessing involves a grandfather who wanted to make sure his grandchildren received this special gift of personal acceptance. Let's look in on this "touching" scene:

> And Joseph said to his father, "They are my sons, whom God has given me in this place." And he said, "Please bring them to me, and I will bless them." Now the eyes of Israel were dim with age, so that he could not see. Then Joseph brought them near him, and he kissed them and embraced them.
>
> Then Israel stretched out his right hand and laid it on Ephraim's head. . . . And his left hand on Manasseh's head (Gen.48:9–10, 14).

Jacob (whose name had now been changed to Israel) not only kissed them and held them close, but he also placed his hands on each grandson's head.[4] This practice of laying on of hands was an important part of many of the religious rituals for the patriarchs and for Israel.

There are at least two important reasons why placing our hands on someone as a part of the blessing is so special. First, there is a symbolic meaning attached to touching, and, second, there are tremendous physical benefits to the laying on of hands.

The Symbolic Meaning Pictured by Touching

In the Old Testament, the symbolic picture of the laying on of hands was important. In this touch was a graphic picture of transferring power or blessing from one person to another.[5] For example, in the Old Testament book of Leviticus Aaron was instructed to use this practice in his priestly duties. During the Day of Atonement, he was to place his hands on the head of a goat that was then sent into the wilderness. This picture is of Aaron symbolically transferring the sins of Israel onto that animal. (It is also a prophetic picture of how Christ, like that spotless animal, would take on our sins at the cross.) In another example, Elijah passed along his role as God's prophet to Elisha by the laying on of hands.

Even today the symbolic meaning of touch is powerful. While we may not be consciously aware of it, the way we touch can carry tremendous symbolic meaning.

A young woman holding hands with a new boyfriend can signal "I'm taken" to other would-be suitors. Two men shaking hands can seal an important business transaction. A minister at a wedding says to a couple, "If you then have freely and lawfully chosen one another as husband and wife, please *join your hands* as you repeat these vows."

Our favorite place to watch the symbolic meaning of touch is in airports. As part of our speaking ministry across the country, both of us spend a lot of time in airports. Sitting in an airport can be a study in human behavior and a study of the powerful symbolic message touch can portray. Here are just a few of the symbolic pictures we see in any given week.

One picture is that of the mother with two young children, keeping an eye on the kids and waiting expectantly for her husband to get off the plane. When he arrives and they hug each other, it is a hug of relief! As she takes her husband's hand, without saying a word, she has the look of "At last, I'm going to have some help with the kids!" In another case, a newly married couple stands far to the rear of those waiting to board the plane. As they hold each other, their embrace says, "I'll miss you. I wish you didn't have to go."

A powerful picture we saw once was an entire family surrounding their oldest son. This young man was in the Army special forces and was heading overseas. Everyone hugged this young man repeatedly, except his father. He would lay his hand on his shoulder and pat him on the back, but he just couldn't bring himself to hug his grown son in public. When it was time for this young soldier to board the plane, his father held out his hand, and the two shook hands.

"Hug him!" we felt like shouting. After a moment, the father took his other hand and placed it around his son's. For what seemed like forever, this father and son stood with their hands clasped, letting this act of touch say their good-byes. Talk about a symbolic message. Even if this father couldn't bring himself to hug his son, he had communicated a great deal. The scene was so powerful. The father's handshake shouted out the words, "I love you. Please, be careful. Come back to us."

When Jacob blessed his grandchildren, they would long remember the symbolic act of his laying his hand on their heads. But symbolism is not the only important reason to touch. Underlying physiological changes happen when we touch as well.

Meaningful Touch Blesses Us Physically

For one thing, over one third of our five million touch receptors are centered in our hands![6] Our hands are so sensitive that some blind people are being taught to read without Braille, by seeing through their fingertips! At Princeton University's Cutaneous Communication Laboratory, "vibratese" is an experimental procedure where blind people are able to read a printed page by translating the words into vibrations on their fingertips.[7]

Interestingly enough, the act of laying on of hands has become the focus of a great deal of modern-day interest and research. Dr. Dolores Krieger, professor of nursing at New York University, has made numerous studies on the effects of laying on of hands. What she found is that both the toucher and the one being touched receive a physiological benefit.[8] How is that possible?

Inside our bodies is hemoglobin, the pigment of the red blood cells, which carries oxygen to the tissues. Repeatedly, Dr. Krieger has found that hemoglobin levels in *both* people's bloodstreams go up during the act of the laying on of hands. As hemoglobin levels are invigorated, body tissues receive more oxygen. This increase of oxygen energizes a person and can even aid in the regenerative process if he or she is ill.

We are sure that Ephraim and Manasseh were not thinking, "Wow, our hemoglobin levels are going up!" when their grandfather laid his hands on them. However, one of the things that certainly stayed with them as they looked back on their day of blessing was the old patriarch's gentle touch.

Hugs and kisses were also a part of meaningful touching pictured in the Scriptures. So healthy is meaningful touch, we ought to listen to the words of Ralph Waldo Emerson: "I never like the giving of the hand, unless the entire body accompanies it!" Let's look further at the physical benefits of touching and the deep emotional needs that can be met by this first element of the family blessing.

How would you like to lower your husband's or wife's blood pressure? Protect your grade-school child from being involved in an immoral relationship later in life? Even add up to two years to your own life? (Almost sounds like an insurance commercial, doesn't it?) Actually, these are all findings in recent studies on the incredible power to bless found in meaningful touching.

MORE REASONS WHY MEANINGFUL TOUCH
BLESSES US PHYSICALLY

Every day, researchers are discovering more and more information about the importance of touch. If we are serious about being a source of blessing to others, we must consider and put into practice these important points. As we saw above in the studies of the laying on of hands, a number of physical changes take place when we reach out and touch. Let's look at a few more of these.

Some nursing homes and animal shelters can be havens of despair, not places of hope. Residents in both can be isolated and alone. Residents in either can spend hours dreaming and longing for a family or friends; and in many cases, the loneliness in an older person's heart can be just as confining as the bars that forsaken animals live behind.

Thankfully, some nursing homes and animal shelters seek to meet their residents' needs. Almost by accident, residents of a nursing home and a local animal shelter were brought together. At first, it was just thought of as a recreational activity for the nursing home patients. Soon, however, more significant results began to surface. Those residents who had a pet to touch and hold not only lived longer than those without, but they also had a significantly more positive attitude about life.[9]

What had changed? The pets still had to go back to the animal shelter, waiting for adoption, and family visits were still nonexistent for many of the elderly. But the few hours when they had someone—even a pet—to touch, to talk to, to love, added new life and energy to those dear, aging folk. We don't usually think of a mutt as being a source of blessing, but for these elderly people they were angels in disguise.

What brought about these physical changes? Studies show that touching can actually lower a person's blood pressure. Low blood pressure is an important part of

staying healthy. But that's not all. In a recent study at
UCLA, it was found that just to maintain emotional and
physical health, men and women need eight to ten meaningful touches each day![10]

At a marriage seminar I (Gary) was conducting, I told
the couples that an important part of the blessing was
given through meaningful touch. When I cited this UCLA
study, I noticed a man in the second row reach over and
begin patting his wife on the shoulder and counting,
"One, two, three . . ." That is not meaningful touching!
These researchers defined meaningful touching as a gentle touch, stroke, kiss, or hug given by significant people
in our lives (a husband or wife, parent, close friend, and
so on).

This study estimated that if some "type A driven" men
would hug their wives several times each day, it would
increase their life span by almost two years! (Not to men-
tion the way it would improve their marriages.) Obviously, we can physically bless those around us (and even
ourselves) with meaningful touch. But touching does
much more than that.

MEANINGFUL TOUCH BLESSES
OUR RELATIONSHIPS

An interesting study done at Purdue University dem-
onstrates how important touch is in determining how we
view someone else. Librarians at the school were asked
by researchers to alternately touch and not touch the
hands of students as they handed back their library
cards. The experimenters then interviewed the students.
Do you know what they found? You guessed it. Those
who had been touched reported far greater positive feelings about both the library and the librarian than those
who were not touched![11]

A doctor we know, a noted neurosurgeon, did his own
study on the effects of brief times of touch. With half his
patients in the hospital, he would sit on their bed and
touch them on the arm or leg when he came in to see how
they were doing. With his remaining patients, he would

simply stand near the bed to conduct his interview of how they were feeling.

Before the patients went home from the hospital, the nurses gave each patient a short questionnaire evaluating the treatment they received. They were especially asked to comment on the amount of time they felt the doctor had spent with them. While in actuality he had spent the same amount of time in each patient's room, those people he had sat down near and touched felt he had been in their room nearly twice as long as those he had not touched!

Come on, Trent. Get serious, Smalley, you may be thinking. Do we really mean that a touch lasting a few seconds or less can help build better relationships? Actually, we hope you touch your loved ones much more than that, but even small acts of touch can indeed leave a lasting memory.

Touching a child on the shoulder when he or she walks in front of you; holding hands with your spouse when you wait in line; stopping for a moment to ruffle someone's hair—all these small acts can change how you are viewed by others. A ten-minute bear hug is not the only way to give another person the blessing. At times, the *smallest* act of touch can be a vehicle to communicating love and personal acceptance.

A free-lance reporter from the *New York Times* was interviewing Marilyn Monroe years ago. She was aware of Marilyn's past and the fact that during her early years Marilyn had been shuffled from one foster home to another. The reporter asked Marilyn, "Did you ever feel loved by any of the foster families with whom you lived?"

"Once," Marilyn replied, "when I was about seven or eight. The woman I was living with was putting on makeup, and I was watching her. She was in a happy mood, so she reached over and patted my cheeks with her rouge puff.... For that moment, I felt loved by her."[12]

Marilyn Monroe had tears in her eyes when she remembered this event. Why? The touch lasted only a few seconds, and it happened years before. It was even done in a casual, playful way, not in an attempt to communicate great warmth or meaning. But as small an act as it was, it was like pouring buckets of love and security on the parched life of a little girl starved for affection.

Parents, in particular, need to know that neglecting to meaningfully touch their children starves them of genuine acceptance—so much so that it can drive them into the arms of someone else who is all too willing to touch them. Analyzing why some young people are drawn to cults, one author writes:

> Cults and related movements offer a new family. They provide the follower with new people to worry about him, to offer him advice, to cry with him, and importantly, to hold him and touch him. Those can be unbeatable attractions.[13]

They certainly can, especially if meaningful touch has not been a part of the blessing a child receives. Even if a child is not lured into a cult to make up for years of touch deprivation, he or she can be drawn into the arms of an immoral relationship.

Promiscuous men and women, women who work as prostitutes, and women who repeatedly have unwanted pregnancies have told researchers that their sexual activity is merely a way of satisfying yearnings to be touched and held. Dr. Marc Hollender, a noted psychiatrist, interviewed scores of women who have had three or more unwanted pregnancies. Overwhelmingly, these women said that they were "consciously aware that sexual activity was a price to be paid for being cuddled and held." Touching before intercourse was more pleasurable than intercourse itself, "which was merely something to be tolerated."[14]

In a similar study with homosexual men, a common characteristic they shared was the absence of meaningful touching by their fathers early in life.[15] Dr. Ross Campbell, in his excellent book, *How to Really Love Your Child*, comes to a similar conclusion. He writes, "In all my reading and experience, I have never known of one sexually disoriented person who had a warm, loving, and affectionate father."[16]

Touch from both a mother and father is important. In a later chapter, we will look at how a single parent can help to make up for the lack of touch from a missing spouse. However, in any case, meaningful touching can protect a child from looking to meet this need in all the wrong places.

If we ignore the physical and emotional needs our children, spouse, or close friends have for meaningful touch, we deny them an important part of the blessing. What's more, we shatter a biblical guideline that our Lord Jesus Himself set in blessing others.

Jesus and the Blessing of Meaningful Touch

As we mentioned in an earlier chapter, Jesus was a model of someone who communicated the blessing to others. Let's look at these verses again that speak of His touching the children.

> Then they brought young children to Him, that He might touch them; but the disciples rebuked those who brought them. But when Jesus saw it, He was greatly displeased and said to them, "Let the little children come to Me, and do not forbid them; for of such is the kingdom of God." And He took them up in His arms, put His hands on them, and blessed them (Mark 10:13–16).

Meaningful touching was certainly a part of Christ's blessing children. Mobbed by onlookers and protected by His disciples, Jesus could have easily waved to the children from a distance or just ignored them altogether. But He did neither. Jesus would not even settle for the politicians' "chuck under the chin" routine; He "took them up in His arms, put His hands on them, and blessed them."

Jesus was not simply communicating a spiritual lesson to the crowds. If He was, He could have done so by simply placing one child in the center of the group as He did on another occasion (Matt. 18:2). Jesus was demonstrating His knowledge of a child's genuine need.

For children, things become real when they are touched. Have you ever been to Disneyland and seen the look on a little child's face when he or she comes face to face with a person dressed like Goofy or Donald Duck? Even if the child is initially fearful, soon he or she will want to reach out and touch the Disney character. This same principle allows children to stand in line for hours to see Santa Claus (the same children who normally can't sit still for five minutes).

Jesus was a master of communicating love and personal acceptance. He did so when He blessed and held these little children. But another time His sensitivity to touch someone was even more graphic. This was when Jesus met a grown man's need for meaningful touch, a man who was barred by law from ever touching anyone again. We read about this in Mark 1:40–42:

> And a leper came to Him, beseeching Him and falling on his knees before Him, and saying to Him, "If you are willing, you can make me clean."
>
> And moved with compassion, *He stretched out His hand and touched him*, and said to him, "I am willing; be cleansed." And immediately the leprosy left him and he was cleansed (NASB, italics added).

To touch a leper was unthinkable. Banishing lepers from society, people would not get within a stone's throw of them. (In fact, they would throw stones at them if they did come close![17]) In a parallel passage in Luke, we are told that this man was "covered with leprosy." With their open sores covered by dirty bandages, lepers were the last persons anyone would want to touch. Yet the first thing Christ did for this man was touch him.

Even before Jesus spoke to him, He reached out His hand and *touched* him. Can you imagine what that scene must have looked like? Think how this man must have longed for someone to touch him, not throw stones at him to drive him away. Jesus could have healed him first and then touched him. But recognizing his deepest need, Jesus stretched out His hand even before He spoke words of physical and spiritual healing.

We know of one person who could understand the pain of not being touched. Her name was Dorothy, and she spent years of her life longing for meaningful touch.

We learned about Dorothy through a speech teacher at a large, secular university. He is a man in his early sixties who is an outstanding Christian. For nearly twenty-five years, this man had been a source of encouragement to students inside and outside of class. Many young men and women have trusted Christ as their Savior through his quiet modeling of godly principles. However, what changed Dorothy's life was neither his ability to communicate nor his stirring class lectures, but one act of touch.

During the first day of an introductory speech class, this teacher was going around the room, having the students introduce themselves. Each student was to respond to the questions "What do I like about myself?" and "What don't I like about myself?"

Nearly hiding at the back of the room was Dorothy. Her long, red hair hung down around her face, almost obscuring it from view. When it was Dorothy's turn to introduce herself, there was only silence in the room. Thinking perhaps she had not heard the question, the teacher moved his chair over near hers and gently repeated the question. Again, there was only silence.

Finally, with a deep sigh, Dorothy sat up in her chair, pulled back her hair, and in the process revealed her face. Covering nearly all of one side of her face was a large, irregularly shaped birthmark—nearly as red as her hair. "That," she said, "should show you what I don't like about myself."

Moved with compassion, this godly professor leaned over and gave her a hug. Then he kissed her on her cheek where the birthmark was and said, "That's OK, Honey, God and I still think you're beautiful."

Dorothy cried uncontrollably for almost twenty minutes. Soon other students had gathered around her and were offering their comfort as well. When she finally could talk, as she dabbed the tears from her eyes she said to the professor, "I've wanted so much for someone to hug me and say what you said. Why couldn't my parents do that? My mother won't even touch my face."

Dorothy, just like the leper in Christ's time, had a layer of inner pain trapped beneath the outward scars. This one act of meaningful touching began to heal years of heartache and loneliness for Dorothy and opened the door that drew her to the Savior.

If we want to be people who give the blessing to others, one thing is clear. Just like Isaac, Jacob, Jesus, and even this professor, we will include meaningful touch in our contacts with loved ones. This element can lay the groundwork for the second key aspect of the blessing—a spoken message.

—4—

The Second Element of the Blessing: Spoken Words

*M*ost of us grew up reciting clever sayings like, "Early to bed, early to rise, makes a man healthy, wealthy, and wise." "A bird in the hand is worth two in the bush." And "A stitch in time saves nine." But unlike all these words of wisdom, one saying we memorized is an absolute lie.

Do you remember the lines, "Sticks and stones may break my bones, but words will never hurt me"? All too quickly we learn that words *do* hurt. They can hurt a person deeply, destroy a friendship, or rip apart a home or marriage.

Words have incredible power to build us up or tear us down emotionally. This is particularly true when it comes to giving or gaining family approval. Many people can clearly remember words of praise their parents spoke years ago. Others can remember negative words they heard—and what their parents were wearing when they spoke them!

We should not be surprised, then, that the family blessing hinges on being a *spoken* message. Abraham *spoke* a blessing to Isaac. Isaac *spoke* it to his son Jacob. Jacob *spoke* it to each of his twelve sons and to two of his grandchildren. Esau was so excited when he was called in to receive his blessing because, after years of waiting, he would finally hear the blessing. In the Scriptures, a blessing is not a blessing unless it is spoken.

The Power of Spoken Words

If you are a parent, your children desperately need to *hear* a spoken blessing from you. If you are married, your wife or husband needs to *hear* words of love and acceptance on a regular basis. This very week with a friend, a co-worker, or someone at your church, you will rub shoulders with someone who needs to hear a word of encouragement.

Throughout the Scriptures, we find a keen recognition of the power and importance of spoken words. In the very beginning, God "spoke" and the world came into being (Gen. 1:3). When He sent us His Son to communicate His love and complete His plan of salvation, it was His Word which "became flesh and dwelt among us" (John 1:14). God has always been a God who communicates His blessings through spoken words.

In the book of James, three word pictures grab our attention and point out the power and importance of spoken words. All three illustrate the ability the tongue has to build up or break down relationships, the ability to bless or to curse.

First, our tongue is pictured as a "bit" used to direct a horse (James 3:3). If you control a horse's mouth by means of a small bit, the entire animal will move in the direction you choose. (We have ridden a few horses who seem to be exceptions, but the general rule is certainly true.) The second picture illustrates this same principle in a different way. Here a "small rudder" is used to turn a great ship (3:4). These analogies point out the way spoken words can direct and control a person or a relationship.

A parent, spouse, or friend can use this power of the tongue for good. He or she can steer a child away from trouble or provide guidance to a friend who is making an important decision. He or she can minister words of encouragement or lift up words of praise. But this power can also be misused, sometimes with tragic results.

That is what the third word picture shows us. It illustrates all too clearly that spoken words can burn deeply into a person's life, often setting the course that person's future will take. Listen to the awesome power a spoken message can have:

> The tongue is a small part of the body, and yet it boasts of great things. Behold, how great a forest is set aflame by such a small fire! And the tongue is a fire, the very world of iniquity; . . . and sets on fire the *course of our life* (James 3:5–6 NASB, italics added).

Just like a forest fire, words can burn deeply into our hearts. In fact, the destructive power of fiery words can affect us for the rest of our lives.

Let us tell you the story of Mean Mike. Actually, this young man's name is only Mike, but his family began calling him this when he was just a toddler. Why "Mean Mike"? Mike had a terrific grip as a young child; and if anyone tried to take something away from him, he would snarl and hold on for dear life. Their nickname of Mean Mike began as a humorous way to picture his bulldog tenacity in holding on to something. But the nickname soon became much more than that; it became the way he lived his life.

When Mean Mike grew older, he became quite a bully at home and at school. Everyone at home still called him "mean," and he lived up to his name. This nickname probably gave him an edge when he played high school football (he was a very good linebacker), but it wreaked havoc in his personal relationships. He was always too tough to get too close to anyone. Little by little, constantly hearing he was mean burned its way into his character.

Today "Mean Mike" is in a state prison in Arizona. Isn't it sad how children can live up to their negative nicknames? Mike certainly did, and it set a tragic course for his life.

Perhaps in your life, you still stumble over hurtful words your parents, spouse, or a close friend spoke to you (or negative words we have spoken to ourselves), words that come to memory time and again and point you in a direction in life you don't want to go. If so, don't lose hope. As you learn more about the blessing, you can begin to hear and speak words that can lead to a new course of life.

Each of us should be keenly aware of the power of spoken words. We should also be aware of how powerful the *absence* of spoken words can be.

"I'll Tell Them Tomorrow": Today's Most Common Choice

In homes like Mike's, negative words can shatter children emotionally rather than shape them positively. But that is not the most common choice of parents. Most parents genuinely love their children and want the best for them. However, when it comes to speaking words of love and acceptance—words of blessing—they are up against an even more formidable foe than the temptation to speak negative words.

A thief is loose in many homes today who masquerades as "fulfillment," "accomplishment," and "success." Actually, this thief steals from our children the precious gift of genuine acceptance and leaves confusion and emptiness in its place. That villain's name is *overactivity*, and it can keep parents so busy that the blessing is never spoken. Even with parents who dearly love their children, as one woman we talked to said, "Who has time to stop and *tell* them?"

In many homes today, both parents are working overtime, and a "family night" makes an appearance about as often as Halley's comet. The result is that instead of Dad and Mom taking the time to communicate a spoken blessing, a babysitter named *silence* is left to mold a child's self-perception. Life is so hectic that for many parents, that "just right" time to communicate a spoken blessing never quite comes around. What is the result?

- A father tries to corner his son to communicate "how he feels about him" before he goes away to college, but now his son is too busy to listen.
- A mother tries to communicate a spoken blessing to her daughter in the bride's room just before the wedding, but the photographer has to take her away to get that "perfect" shot.

Spoken words of blessing should start in the delivery room and continue throughout life. Yet the "lack of time" and the thief's motto, "I'll have time to tell them tomorrow," rob children of a needed blessing today.

"Oh, it's not that big a deal," you may say. "They know I love them and that they're special *without* my having to say it." Really? We wish that explanation worked with many of the people we counsel. To them, their parents' silence has communicated something far different from love and acceptance.

Let's look at what commonly happens in homes where spoken words of blessing are withheld. What we will see is that silence does communicate a message; and like an eloquent speech, silence too can set a course for a person's life. But it's not the path most parents would like their children to take. In fact, for many, silence affects their every relationship and leaves them wandering between workaholism and extreme withdrawal.

What Happens When We Withhold Words of Blessing?

Both people and relationships suffer in the absence of spoken words of love, encouragement, and support—words of blessing. Take a marriage, for example.

Dr. Howard Hendricks, a noted Christian educator, is fond of telling the story of a couple he counseled several years ago. This couple had been married over twenty years, but their problems had become so acute they were now considering divorce. Dr. Hendricks asked the husband, "When was the last time you told your wife you loved her?" The man glared at him, crossed his arms, and said, "I told my wife I loved her on our wedding day, and it stands until I revoke it!"

Take a guess what was destroying their marriage. When a spoken blessing is withheld in a marriage, unmet needs for security and acceptance act like sulfuric acid and eat away at a relationship.

Not only marriages, but individuals—particularly children—suffer from the lack of a spoken blessing. Without words of love, acceptance, and encouragement, children often grow up traveling one of two roads that lead to unhealthy extremes. Take Dan, for example. He took the road marked, "Try a little harder, maybe that will get you the blessing."

TAKING THE ROAD TO WORKAHOLISM

Dan grew up in a home where nothing positive was ever said. In fact, little of *anything* was ever said. His parents seemed too busy with their careers or too preoccupied with constantly "remodeling" the house to do much talking. There came, however, an exception to the general rule of indifference when Dan was just a boy.

At the end of one semester in grade school, Dan received an excellent report card with nearly all *A*'s. For the first time in memory, his parents openly spoke words of praise. At last, he felt like a somebody.

Like a starving man who stumbles across a loaf of bread, Dan thought he had learned the key to hearing words of acceptance: *overachieve*. Acceptance was worth the hours spent inside studying (with the neighbor kids playing right outside his window) just to hear a few words of affirmation at the end of a semester. This working to overachieve lasted right through college.

The only problem Dan had was that his need for words of acceptance outlasted the years he spent in school. As a result, he took his motivation to "show them I'm somebody" right into the marketplace. Naturally, Dan became a "perfect" junior executive (which translated means he was a committed workaholic, always driven to achieve more and more regardless of the personal or relationship costs).

Why the intense drive and the insatiable need to achieve? Just look back at Dan's home, where no spoken blessing was given—except for some spectacular achievement. While Dan would never admit it (but inside he always knew it), pulling into his parents' driveway in a new car said he was still a somebody—didn't it? Getting that corner office would show them—wouldn't it?

Gordon MacDonald, in his excellent book and film series *Ordering Your Private World,* does a beautiful job of picturing a driven man or woman. Dan met every qualification. He had fallen into the trap many men and women do who never received the blessing. Like Moses' fading glory, accomplishments could not sustain a missing sense of personal acceptance. Dan was forever having to make one more deal, sell one more product, attend one more motivational seminar. Spoken words of love and acceptance went unsaid early in Dan's life; as a result, his search for acceptance left him at the door of the driven.[1]

To borrow a phrase from MacDonald's book, a key to bringing order into Dan's private world was when he finally came to grips with missing out on the blessing. Until then, his search for personal acceptance kept him on the barren road to success and away from the pathway of life.

TAKING THE ROAD OF WITHDRAWAL

Many people who missed out on hearing words of blessing take another road. These people head in the opposite direction. Convinced they can do nothing to hear words of love and acceptance, they give up and travel down the road of apathy, depression, and withdrawal. At the end of the road of withdrawal can be a terrifying, yet beckoning, cliff.

A classic example of a child who took this road is found in a film that circulated several years ago. As the movie begins, we see several children waiting for their school bus. The sun is out on a cold January morning. Snow covers the rural countryside like a beautiful, white blanket.

All bundled up for winter weather, a few of the children are making snowballs and throwing them at a fence. Others laugh and talk and stomp their feet trying to stay warm. All except Roger.

Standing by himself at the edge of the group, Roger stares down at the ground. In the next few moments, you almost get the feeling that Roger is invisible. Several children run right by him in excited conversation; others crowd around him when the bus finally comes. But Roger never looks up, and the other children never speak to him or acknowledge his existence.

The children rush to see who gets on the school bus first. Glad to be in out of the cold, the children happily take their seats—that is, all except Roger. The last one on the bus, he wearily mounts the steps as if climbing each one requires a monumental effort. He stops briefly and looks up expectantly into the faces of the other children, but no one beckons him to join them. Heaving a sigh, he slumps into a seat behind the driver.

The sound of compressed air is heard being released from the bus's hydraulic system, and the door slams shut. With one look behind him to make sure everything is in order, the bus driver pulls slowly away from the curb and onto the country lane.

They have traveled only a few miles when suddenly Roger drops his books and staggers to his feet. Standing next to the bus driver, steadying himself on a metal pole, Roger has a wild and distant look in his eyes. Shocked by his sudden ill appearance, the bus driver asks, "Are you all right? Are you sick or something? Kid, what's the matter?" Roger never answers, and half out of frustration, half out of concern, the bus driver pulls over to the side of the road and opens the door.

As Roger begins to walk down the steps of the bus, he pitches forward and crumples into the snow. As the opening scene ends, we see the bus driver standing over Roger's body, trying to discover what has happened. As the camera pulls away, we hear an ambulance siren begin to whine in the distance, but somehow you know its coming will be too late.

This scene is from the excellent educational film *A Cipher in the Snow*, a film designed for teachers but that speaks to anyone concerned about giving the blessing to others. The movie is a true story of a young boy who actually died on the way to school one day and the resulting confusion over the reasons.

Medical records indicated no history of problems in either Roger or his family. Even the autopsy shed no light on his death. Only after an interested teacher looked into his school and family background were the reasons for his death discovered.

This teacher found that Roger's life had been systematically erased like a blackboard. In his first few years at school, he had done well, up until problems began at home. His parents' marriage had disintegrated, and a new, preoccupied stepfather never had time to fill any of the missing gaps. Resentful of any attention his new wife gave Roger, the stepfather would limit their time together. His mother loved Roger dearly, but soon she was either too busy or too intimidated by her new husband to give Roger any attention at all. Like being pushed away from a seat near the fireplace, Roger was now left with only the cold ache of indifference.

As a reaction to his home life, Roger's school work began to suffer. Homework assignments were either turned in late or not at all. Tired of his apparent apathy, his teachers gave up on him and left him to work alone. He also began to withdraw from the other children at school, and he lost the few friends he once had. Roger would not begin a conversation, and soon other children wouldn't bother to try. Slowly but surely he was retreating into a world of silence.

In only a few months, everything and everyone of value to Roger had either been lost or taken from him. With no place of shelter and no words of encouragement, he felt like a cipher—an empty zero. This sensitive child was unable to stand the pain for long.

Roger was not killed by an infirmity nor a wound. He was killed by a lack of words of love and acceptance. Roger withstood the painful silence as long as he could. Ultimately, however, the lack of a spoken blessing from family and friends acted like a deadly cancer. After months of pursuing its course, it finally ate away his will to live. He died a cipher in the snow, believing he was totally alone and unwanted.

Are words or their absence *really* that powerful? Solomon thought so. Like throwing ice water in our faces, he shocks us into reality with his words, "Death and life are in the power of the tongue" (Prov. 18:21).

If we struggle with speaking words of love and acceptance to our family or friends, another proverb should encourage us. Again, it is Solomon writing:

> Do not withhold good from those to whom it is due when it is in the power of your hand to do so. Do not say, . . . "Go, and come back, and tomorrow I will give it," when you have it with you (Prov. 3:27–28).

If we can open our mouths to talk, we have the ability to communicate the blessing by spoken words. By deciding to communicate words of love and acceptance verbally, we do not have to send away a child, spouse, or friend in need.

Why Is It So Hard to Speak Words of Blessing?

The damage of withholding words of blessing should be obvious in the examples of Mike, Dan, and Roger. But if spoken words of love and acceptance are so important, why are they offered so infrequently? Here are a few reasons we have gathered from people we have counseled:

"I don't want to inflate my child's ego."

"I'm afraid if I praise them, they'll take advantage of me and won't finish their work."

> "Communication is too much like work. I work all day, then she expects me to work all night talking to her."
>
> "I just don't know what to say."
>
> "They know I love them without my having to say it."
>
> "If I get started, I'll have to make a habit of it."

Our favorite reason is this one:

> "Telling children their good points is like putting on perfume. A little is OK; but put on too much and it stinks."

If the truth be known, the reason many people hesitate to bless their children or others with spoken words of love and acceptance is that their parents never gave them this part of the blessing.

Beware of Some Family Rules

Both praise and criticism seem to trickle down through generations. If you never heard words of love and acceptance, expect to struggle with speaking them yourself. Why? If your family had a "rule" that loving words were best left unsaid, you may find it very difficult to break this rule.

Every family operates by certain "rules." These rules make up "the way our family does things." Some families have a rule that "people who know anything about anything" open Christmas presents on *Christmas morning*. Other families follow the rule that "truly civilized people" open Christmas presents on *Christmas Eve*. (Both our wives, Cindy and Norma, just groaned when we wrote this!) Conflicting family rules often meet in a marriage. Many an argument has gone fifteen rounds to see whose family rule will win out in a new marriage.

Families set all kinds of rules: What we will eat in this family, and what we won't eat. What television programs we can watch, and which are dull or off limits. What is safe to talk about, and what subjects should never be brought up. Whom we invite over to the house, and who doesn't get an invitation.

In some cases family rules can be very helpful. For example, families can adopt biblical rules like "not letting the sun go down on our anger" and "being kind, one to another." Another way of setting positive family rules is by using "contracts" that can help build communication and encourage your children.[2] These types of family guidelines can be safely passed down generation after generation.

But not all family rules are worth retaining. Some family rules—written or unwritten—can devastate a family. Like words cast in steel, a destructive family rule can hammer away at a family, from parent to son or daughter, until at last someone breaks this painful pattern, someone like Cherryl.

When Cherryl was growing up, a simple plaque hung in the family room. The plaque had belonged to Cherryl's grandfather and had become a kind of unspoken "family motto." The plaque was not impressive looking, and it carried only two hand-painted words: STAND UP. Just two words—yet these two words had written volumes of hurt into three generations of Cherryl's family.

The words were originally part of a longer sentence, a motto that went something like this: "Don't take anything off anyone. Stand up and fight." This slogan may have been a helpful frontier slogan, but it did nothing but damage to personal relationships in Cherryl's family. Just look at Cherryl's father.

Cherryl's father had been infected with the "never give an inch" attitude of *his* father. "I'm sorry" or "You're right" were not in the vocabulary of someone who based his life on the words "Stand up and fight." Also absent were words that were not useful in a fight. Words like "I love you," "Will you forgive me?" and "You're important to me." While following this family rule of "never give an inch" pushed Cherryl's father ahead in business, it pushed him back into a corner with his wife and children.

Cherryl's mother and father fought constantly, each

an expert on the other's faults, neither willing to give an inch in an argument. When each of Cherryl's four brothers and sisters grew old enough to dislike "taking orders" from their father, they joined the battle too. Soon there were seven people under the same roof following the family rule of "Stand up and fight" and its corollary principles, "Fight for my rights" and "Death before saying I'm sorry." This situation was true until Cherryl became a Christian.

Cherryl went away to a Young Life camp and trusted Christ as her Lord and Savior. The first thing Cherryl noticed when she came back home were those two words, "Stand Up." She thought about how Jesus had laid down His life and how tired she was of following this family rule. Little by little, and at the painful cost of constant ridicule from her brothers and sisters, Cherryl began to break several family rules.

Right in the middle of a fight, Cherryl would say, "I'm sorry; you're right. Would you forgive me?" and end the argument. She even began saying, "Love you, Mom, love you, Dad," and then giving them a hug as she left for school.

Cherryl's father had never gotten the blessing from his parents, only a plaque that almost destroyed his marriage and family. But over the next two years, he received the blessing from Cherryl. Meaningful touch, spoken words of high value, the picture of a future filled with hope, and the commitment to love him, no matter the cost—all these were relationship tools that chipped away at their existing family structure.

Family rules die hard, but they can be broken. Cherryl's younger sister was so taken with Cherryl's changed life that she also trusted Christ. Soon Cherryl's older brother followed, and the plaque on the wall was beginning to shake. Last Christmas, as a baby Christian, her father took down the plaque.

What a testimony to God's power to break even the most difficult family rule! And what a help to Cherryl's family to have a new family rule to follow! They are now free to "speak up" and share words of blessing with each other—because of one child's courage to go to battle with a hurtful rule of silence.

Putting Words of Blessing into Practice

We put spoken words of blessing into practice in our homes and relationships by deciding to speak up rather than clam up. Good intentions aside, good words are needed to bestow the blessing on a child, spouse, or friend.

We are not simply saying talk more to your children or others. While that is normally a good idea, sometimes if you don't know how to communicate in a positive way, you can say less by saying more. As we will see in the next chapter, it is not just *any* words, but words of high value, that attach themselves to a person and communicate the blessing. These are the kinds of words you often hear in the final hours before a family reunion ends.

Almost all of us have had the opportunity to attend a family reunion. A common phenomenon at these gatherings is that during the first two days, everyone is busy talking up a storm about this recipe, that football team, this book they've read, or that movie to attend. But something happens the last afternoon of the reunion. Suddenly with only an hour left before family members say their good-byes, meaningful words will begin to be spoken.

A brother will say in private to his sister, "I know things will work out in your marriage. I'll be praying for you." An aunt will say to her niece, "You've always made me proud. I know school is hard, but I know you can do it. I believe in you." Or a daughter will say to a parent, "Look around you, Mom. We didn't turn out half bad, did we? We have you and Dad to thank."

Spoken words—many times we have to be facing the pressure of time before we say the things closest to our hearts. What we have tried to communicate in this chap-

ter is that with your children, your spouse, your close friends, even with your parents, it's later than you think. In some relationships, it is already late afternoon in your opportunity to talk to them.

At the time we were writing this chapter, a tragic airplane crash in Japan took the lives of over five hundred people. Four people survived the crash, and they told authorities and reporters the story of the tragic last half hour of their doomed flight. For thirty-four minutes, the plane was without a rear tail stabilizer to control their descent. As a result, the erratic descent of the airplane was a time of panic and horror for all on board. While some passengers cried in fear and others took the time to don life jackets, one middle-aged Japanese man, Hirotsugu Kawaguchi, took his last few moments of life to write a note to his family. His note was found on his body by rescuers at the wreckage site, and it finally made its way to his wife and three children.

Listen to the last words of this man who deeply loved his family. They picture his desire for his wife and children to have a special future, even now that they would be physically separated in this life.

> I'm very sad, but I'm sure I won't make it. The plane is rolling around and descending rapidly. There was something like an explosion that has triggered smoke. . . . Ysuyoshi [his oldest son], I'm counting on you. You and the other children be good to each other, and work hard. Remember to help your mother. . . . Keiko [his wife], please take good care of yourself and the children. To think our dinner last night was our last. I am grateful for the truly happy life I have enjoyed. . . .[3]

This man's wife and children no longer have him to hold and love. Hirotsugu Kawaguchi died when the plane crashed. But they do have his final words to them, words that pictured his hopes for their future, and words that will echo in their lives in a positive way in the years to come.

In the next chapter, you can learn about the *kind* of

words—words of high value—that can especially bless people, but don't delay. Time passes so quickly. Please don't let that important person leave your life without hearing the second element of the blessing—spoken words.

—5—

The Third Element of the Blessing: Expressing High Value

━━━━━━━━━━ ✍ ━━━━━━━━━━

*D*iane's parents had tried unsuccessfully for years to have children. Perhaps that is one reason why their joy was unbounded when they learned that they were carrying their first child. Everything seemed normal during the pregnancy and delivery, until they saw the doctor's reactions. When Diane was given to them for the first time they saw that her left arm had never developed below the elbow.

There were tears in the delivery room and deep concern as test after test was performed on Diane. As doctors and specialists sought to determine the extent of her physical problems, Diane's parents didn't know how they should handle the anxious questions from relatives and friends.

Two days later, the doctors told Diane's parents some encouraging news. In all their tests, they had not picked up any other signs of medical or physical problems. Diane appeared to be a normal, healthy baby girl, with the exception of her left arm.

After the doctors had gone, Diane's parents bowed together in prayer. They thanked God that their daughter had no other serious problems. But they prayed something else that proved to be of tremendous benefit to their daughter. In that hospital room, with Diane nestled in her mother's arms, her parents prayed that their love for her would make up for any lack of physical abilities she possessed. They decided that morning that they would encourage Diane to become all that God would have her be, in spite of the problems they and Diane would have to face along the way.

Years have gone by since Diane's parents prayed for her in that hospital room. In fact, Diane is nineteen now and attending a major university. However, something special about Diane draws your attention away from her empty sleeve, particularly when you listen to her play a beautiful melody on the piano—with only one hand.

Diane has had to deal with tremendous obstacles in her nineteen years. The stares, giggles, and tactless questions of her peers in grade school; the fears and uncomfortable feelings of whether to go to a dance in junior high; the questions and worry that perhaps she would never date in high school, just to name a few. On the other hand, throughout the real-life struggles of being born handicapped, Diane received a precious and powerful gift from her parents—the security of knowing she was highly valued and unconditionally accepted.

"My parents didn't try to hide from me the fact that I was different," Diane told us. "They have been very realistic with me. But I always knew, and they have told me over and over that 'I am their greatest claim to fame.' Whether I was trying out for softball or my dad was teaching me how to drive, they have been my biggest fans. They have prayed for me and thought the best, even when I've pouted and gotten angry at God because of my handicap. Without question, my parents deserve a lot of credit for helping me accomplish the things I have."

They certainly do. Credit for deciding, in spite of a physical deformity, to value their daughter as whole and complete. Diane's parents are realists. They have not sugar-coated the very real problems their daughter has faced. But for nineteen years, they have communicated the blessing to her by showering her with words of high value and unconditional acceptance.

Words of High Value

What do we mean by "high value"? Let's look at the word *value* to see the part it plays in the blessing.

As we mentioned in an earlier chapter, to "value" something means to attach great importance to it.[1] This is at the very heart of the concept of "blessing." In Hebrew, to "bow the knee" is the root meaning of blessing.[2] This root word is used of a man who had his camel bend its knees so he could get on (Gen. 24:11). In relationship to God the word came to mean "to adore with bended knees."[3] Bowing before someone is a graphic picture of valuing that person. Notice the important principle here: Anytime we bless someone, we are attaching high value to him or her. Let's illustrate this by an example in my (Gary's) home.

In my life, I want God to be of utmost value to me. He is my best friend and the source of my life. If I were to chart this on a 1-to-10 scale, I would value the Lord at "10," of highest value. Right beneath my relationship with the Lord would come my relationship with Norma, my wife. Humanly speaking, she is my best friend, and I love and value her right beneath my love for the Lord, maybe a "9.5." Then come my children. I love each of them dearly, and while neither they nor Norma are aware that I love them at a different level, I would value them at about a "9.4," right behind Norma. I do not love them less; but in attaching value to them, they come right behind my relationship with my Lord and with my wife.

Now I need to be honest with you. Emotionally, there are times with the kids when my feelings for them might drop to a "6.4" or even a "4.2." Particularly if we are camping in our mini-mobile home, and it has been raining all week. But, because I want to love and value them at a "9.4," I continually try to push their value back where it belongs. The same thing is true with Norma. I don't want to hurt or devalue her in any way. That is why if I do offend her, I immediately decide to raise her value to just beneath where I value the Lord. How does this apply to the blessing?

This principle is so important, let's repeat it. When we bless someone, we are deciding that he or she is of high value. This is what the psalmist is telling us in Psalm 103 when he says, "Bless the Lord, O my soul, and all that is within me bless His holy Name." When we "bless the Lord," we are actually recognizing God's instrinic worth and attaching high value to Him. He is worthy of our "bowing the knee" to Him.[4]

In the Scriptures, we are often called on to bless or value the Lord; but the Scriptures also give many examples of men blessing other men (Deut. 33:1, 2; Josh. 14:13; 2 Sam. 6:18) and others. When they did, they were attaching high value to the person they were blessing. They were recognizing him or her as a very special individual.

This valuing is exactly what the patriarchs in the Old Testament did in blessing their children with the family blessing. They were attaching high value to them. We do the same thing when we bless our children, spouse, or friends, and every person today needs the blessing to feel truly loved and secure about himself or herself. This concept of valuing another person is so important that we believe it can be found at the heart of every healthy relationship.

Words of High Value in Old Testament Homes

In the Old Testament, shining threads of love and value run throughout the fabric of the blessing. We can see this in the words Isaac spoke to Jacob: "Surely, the smell of my son / Is like the smell of a field / Which the LORD has blessed. . . . / Let the peoples serve you, / And nations bow down to you" (Gen. 27:27–28 NASB).

Telling your children today that they "smell like a

field" would probably not be seen as a compliment! But Jacob knew what his father meant. So can you if you remember driving through the country when hay or wheat has been harvested recently. Particularly with the morning dew on the ground, or after a rain shower, the smell of a newly cut field is as fresh and refreshing as a mountain spring.

Isaac also pictured his son as someone that other people, including his own family, should greatly respect. He was even someone who deserved to be "bowed down to" by nations because he was valuable.

In the United States, no premium is placed on bowing before dignitaries. About the only people who know how to bow anymore are orchestra conductors and high school debutantes. Most of us would have to practice for hours to properly bow if we were going to meet a visiting king or queen. In Isaac's day, to bow the knee was a mark of respect and honor, something that was expected in the presence of an important person.

We can't miss the idea in these two pictures of praise that Jacob's father thought he was very valuable, someone who had great worth. This message is exactly what modern-day children need to hear from their parents. This message is what Diane received and what caused her life to blossom and grow, in spite of her physical deformity.

Word Pictures: Helpful Tools for Communicating Value to Others

Telling children they are valuable can be difficult for many parents. As we saw in the last chapter, that just right time to say such important words can get crowded out by the urgent demands of a busy schedule. Some parents do struggle through the obligatory "I love you" during holidays or at the airport; but it seems stiff and out of place.

Other children may hear an occasional word of praise, but only if they perform well on a task (like Dan's story in the previous chapter). When words of value are only linked to a child's performance, they lose much of their impact. Children who have to perform to get a blessing retain a nagging uncertainty about whether they ever really received it. If their performance ever drops even a small amount, they can ask and re-ask, "Am I loved for 'who I am' or only for 'what I can do'?"

We need to find a better way to communicate a message of high value and acceptance, a way to picture a person's valuable qualities and character traits apart from his or her performance. Hidden inside the family blessing is a key to communicating such feelings to our children, spouse, friends, or church family, a key we can perfect with only a little practice, and one that even gets around the walls a defensive adult or child can set up. This key is found in the way word pictures are used throughout the Scriptures.

We may not be aware of it, but we use word pictures all the time. Let me give you one example of a word picture that I (John) remember vividly.

I was at lunch some time ago with a close friend in Dallas, Texas. We were eating at a quaint little basement restaurant where you walk down a steep flight of steps to reach the front door. The hostess seated us, and from our table we had a view of the stairs leading down to the restaurant. That is when it happened.

While we were waiting for our meal, we noticed at the top of the stairs a little girl of about two. She was holding on to someone's hand who as yet we could not completely see. In fact, all we could see were two huge tennis shoes and a massive hand holding on to this little girl. As these two came down the stairs, we were able to see more and more of this very large man helping his little daughter down the stairs.

When they reached the foot of the stairs and the door to the restaurant opened, in walked a pro football player for the Dallas Cowboys. At 6'4" and 265 pounds, this huge defensive tackle took up nearly the whole doorway! As he and his daughter walked by our table (the ground shaking and plates rattling on our table as he walked by), my friend leaned over to me and said, "Boy, what a moose!"

Calling this man a moose is using a word picture. Randy White does not have antlers and fur; and while he is very large as far as human beings go, he does not outweigh even a baby moose. Yet by picturing him as a moose (when he couldn't hear us do it of course), I instantly knew what my friend was talking about: a very large individual was walking by our table!

Some men have called attractive women chicks down through the years. Obviously, they do not refer to the fact that they scratch around in the dirt. A junior high school girl who tells her girlfriends that her latest boyfriend is a dream before she goes to sleep at a slumber party does not mean he will evaporate when she wakes up (even if it frequently happens!). Each of these "word pictures" captures an emotional feeling apart from the literal meaning of the words.

Now, let's look at the Scriptures and the blessing Jacob used with three of his sons. Each is a beautiful example of how this communication tool can be used to communicate high value to a child.

Word from the Wise

Judah is a lion's cub . . . and as a lion, who dares rouse him up?

Naphtali is a doe let loose, he gives beautiful words.

Joseph is a fruitful bough, a fruitful bough by a spring (Gen. 49:9, 21, 22 NASB).

Jacob used a different word picture with each of his sons to bestow the blessing. We read, "And that is what their father said to them when he blessed them. He blessed them, every one with the blessing appropriate to him" (49:28).

Judah was depicted as a "lion's cub." In the Scriptures, a lion portrayed strength and was also a symbol of royalty in the ancient Near East.[5] The leadership qualities and strength of character Judah possessed were illustrated by this word picture.

Jacob pictured Naphtali as a "doe." The grace and beauty of this gentle animal were used to show the artistic qualities this son possessed. He was the one who spoke and wrote beautiful words.

Finally, Joseph was called a "fruitful bough by a spring." This word picture illustrated how Joseph's unfailing trust in the Lord resulted in his providing a place of refuge for his family. Jacob's word picture carries a similar message to one used first of Jesus in Psalm 1:3: "And he will be like a tree planted by streams of water, Which yields its fruit in its season, and its leaf does not wither; and in whatever he does, he prospers" (NASB).

Each of Jacob's sons was an individual, and each of them received a blessing that depicted his value to his father in the form of a word picture he could remember always.

Before we rush off to call our child or spouse a lion, doe, or someone filled with fruit, we need to learn a little more about word pictures. To do so, let's turn to a book in the Old Testament that is filled with them. Word pictures can be used in any relationship to communicate words of high value. While this book pictures a marriage relationship, the same principles are used in giving children the blessing. Let's look in on how this couple communicated words of love, acceptance, and praise. In doing so, we will discover four keys to communicating high value.

Word Pictures: Four Keys to Communicating High Value

In the Song of Solomon, God's picture of an ideal courtship and marriage, this loving couple praise each other using word pictures over eighty times in eight short chapters. That's a lot! But they had a lot they wanted to communicate about how highly they valued each other and their relationship.

Let's begin our look at how they used these descriptive words with each other by looking in on their wedding night. Not often is someone's wedding night written up for posterity, but this one is worth remembering. It is a loving record of a godly relationship.[6]

Seven times Solomon praises his bride (the biblical number of perfection). She was altogether beautiful to him. He begins his praise of her by saying, "Behold, you are fair, my love! / Behold, you are fair! / You have dove's eyes behind your veil" (Song of Sol. 4:1).

THE FIRST KEY: USE AN EVERYDAY OBJECT

What Solomon does with his word picture (and what a wise parent does in blessing his or her child) is to try to capture a character trait or physical attribute of his beloved in an everyday object. In this case, he pictures her eyes as dove's. The gentle, shy, and tender nature of these creatures would be familiar to his bride. By using a familiar object, Solomon is able to communicate far more meaning using a picture than he could by using mere words. Spoken words are often one-dimensional, but a word picture can be multidimensional. Plus, an added feature is that each time she saw a dove thereafter, it would remind her of how her husband viewed her and valued her.

Let's look at how one young woman's parents used an everyday object in a blessing to their daughter and how it ministered to her life. While Christmas doesn't come every day, their choice of an object was familiar to their loved one.

Nancy was born in late December, near Christmas day. As she grew older, her parents would repeatedly say to her, "Just remember, you're God's special Christmas gift to us, a gift of great price because you're so special to us." As a way of illustrating their feelings, each Christmas (now for almost thirty-five years), a small package is placed under the Christmas tree addressed from Jesus to Nancy's parents. Each year, Nancy is given the honor of opening this package. Inside the package is her baby picture! Listen to Nancy's thoughts about how being called a Christmas gift over the years has ministered to her.

"There have been many times when I haven't felt very special. I can remember one time in particular. It was my thirtieth birthday, and I was really struggling with growing older. When I was at my lowest point, I received a package in the mail from my parents. In the package was a brightly wrapped box, and inside was my baby picture and a note from my parents. I've always known I was special to them. But I *needed* to know I was special that day. It wasn't even Christmas, but reading again that I was their special 'Christmas gift' and very special to them— even on my thirtieth birthday—filled my heart with love and warmth."

THE SECOND KEY: MATCH THE EMOTIONAL MEANING OF THE TRAIT YOU ARE PRAISING WITH THE OBJECT YOU'VE PICKED

Over and over Solomon uses everyday objects that capture the emotional meaning behind the trait he wants to praise. These objects may not be familiar to us, but they were familiar to his bride. Take, for example, his praise for his beloved just a few verses later.

Solomon looks at his bride and says, "Your neck is like the tower of David, / Built for an armory / On which hang a thousand bucklers / All shields of mighty men" (4:4). Was Solomon trying to end his marriage before it began? Certainly not. Let's look at just how meaningful this analogy would have been to an insecure, blushing bride on her wedding night.

High above the old city of Jerusalem stood the Tower of David. A farmer working outside the city walls could look up from his work and see this imposing structure. However, what would impress him even more than the height of this tower was what was hanging on it.

Hanging on this tower during times of peace were the war shields of David's "mighty men." The mighty men were King David's greatest warriors and the leaders of his armies. Looking up at the sun shining off their shields would be a reassuring sight for one outside the protection of the city walls. By the same token, if that farmer looked up and the shields of the mighty men had been taken off the tower, he would know it was time to hightail it inside the city walls! Danger was in the land.

Solomon's comparing David's tower to his bride's neck now begins to make more sense. In Old Testament times a person's neck stood for his or her appearance *and* attitude. That is why the Lord would call a disobedient Israel a "stiff-necked people" (Exod. 33:5). For Solomon, the peace and security represented in David's tower provided a powerful illustration to express his love for his bride. He was praising the way she carried herself; with serenity and security.[7]

Let's give a modern-day example to reinforce what we have discovered about word pictures so far. One mother we taught about the blessing noticed how helpful and protective her oldest daughter had been with her little brother and sister. The mother decided to try to think of a creative way she could communicate words of high value to her daughter.

First, she looked around for an everyday object that represented some of those same characteristics (the first key to using word pictures). Her eyes fell on "Mama Kitty," the family cat looking after a recent litter of kittens. Mama Kitty would nurse and tend her kittens with all the attention of a loving mother. This mother cat's care was a beautiful illustration of the emotional side to caring and protecting (the second key to using word pictures).

Bringing her daughter to where she could see the mama cat and her kittens, she said, "Sweetheart, I'm so proud of you. You remind me of Mama Kitty the way you look out for your little brother and sister." The woman's daughter beamed at her mother's words. This girl had frequently watched the way Mama Kitty had taken care of her young, and she knew exactly what her mother meant. By using an everyday object to picture her praise, this wise mother communicated even more than a simple

compliment. She also gave her daughter a living illustration she could see of how valuable she was to her mother.

A THIRD KEY: WORD PICTURES
UNRAVEL OUR DEFENSES

Solomon gained a third thing by using word pictures
that a parent, spouse, or friend can also use today. What
he gained is the ability word pictures have to get around
the defenses of insecure or defensive people and to get
across a message of high value. Let's look first at how a
word picture can encourage an insecure person. We can
see this with Solomon's bride herself, and it can be a
valuable lesson to anyone who has a loved one who struggles with accepting herself or himself.

Like most young women who would unexpectedly
meet a dashing young king, the Shulamite woman was
insecure about her appearance. When she first meets
Solomon she says, "Do not look upon me, because I am
dark, / Because the sun has tanned me" (1:6). But after
she had been around Solomon for only a short time, she
calls herself, "The rose of Sharon, the lily of the valley"
(2:1). That is quite a change of perspective! How did it
happen?

In spite of herself, Solomon's word pictures made
their way around his bride's defenses. If Solomon had
simply said, "You're cute," her insecurity could have
thrown up a dozen reasons why this matter-of-fact statement could not be true: "Maybe his eyesight is bad." "I
bet he's been hunting for three months, and I'm the first
woman he's seen." "Maybe my father paid him to say
that." These same kinds of reasons are used by insecure
people today to ward off any compliments they hear
about themselves. But word pictures capture our attention in spite of our defenses.

We will listen to praise more intently when it comes
packaged in a word picture. That is one reason why our
Lord used word pictures to communicate both praise
and condemnation through the parables. These extended
object lessons kept his audience's attention, even if, like

the Pharisees, they really didn't want to hear what he was saying!

Jesus knew the importance of using word pictures with those who were timid of heart. He would talk about being the Good Shepherd who watched over the flock; the true vine that could bring spiritual sustenance; and the bread of life that would provide spiritual nourishment. By using everyday objects, He was able to penetrate the walls of insecurity and mistrust these people had put up, because stories hold a key to our hearts that simple words do not.

How do we know word pictures really got through to Solomon's bride in their marriage? Just look at how her attitude changed over the course of their married life.

During their courtship, she viewed their relationship with a certain insecurity and possessiveness. These feelings are evident in the way she talks about their relationship saying, *"My beloved is mine, and I am his"* (2:16).

As their story continues after their wedding—and as she grows more secure in his love—watch the subtle but powerful change in how she views their relationship. Once they are married, in speaking to the ladies of the court she says, *"I am my beloved's, and my beloved is mine"* (6:3). This statement shows a little more security.

Then, as their story draws to a close, she even says, *"I am my beloved's, and his desire is toward me"* (7:10, italics added). This final statement shows a lot more security than her view of their relationship just before their wedding night. Why? The major reason is the way word pictures of praise and great value have brought security to an insecure woman's heart. Repeatedly (over fifty times), Solomon expressed his high value for his bride by using word pictures. Something parents and even friends can effectively use today in praising an insecure person.

As we mentioned above, word pictures can also be used with people who may not be insecure, but are defensive when it comes to what we want to tell them. Let us illustrate how one word picture got around the defenses of a couple that was struggling in their marriage and literally changed their relationship for the better.

I (Gary) was counseling a young couple who had been having heated arguments for a long period of time. Things had become so strained between Bill and Barb that they had even considered separating. They were angry and defensive when they walked into the office. Sitting with their arms crossed looking straight ahead, each of their nonverbals was saying "You just try and say something to change my mind. I'm walking out of this marriage."

Bill was a rugged outdoorsman who had moved his family outside the city limits so he would be closer to the hunting and fishing he loved. He didn't mind the thirty-five-mile drive to work each day as long as he could live in the wilderness. At first, his wife had liked joining him on his backpacking trips; but with two young children, now he did all his camping alone.

Barb was a petite, city girl who enjoyed socializing. With the move out of town, she was now an hour from her closest friend. The only socializing she did during the day was with two toddlers. While Barb loved her children deeply, being isolated from her friends and having a husband who hunted or fished every spare minute was leading her to become bitter and resentful.

After listening to them talk for more than an hour about how insensitive the other person was, I shared with them this word picture that opened their eyes to a completely new way of viewing each other.

"Let me close our time together by telling you two a word picture that comes to my mind as I have listened to you talk. Bill, I could see you as a picture, hanging on a wall, of a mighty stag with a huge rack of antlers. You are standing proudly near a mountain stream, looking over the forest, with your doe and newborn fawns in the background. The square frame around the picture is heavy and made out of antique wood.

"Barb, I see you as a picture of a delicate, beautiful wildflower with dazzling colors and fine brush strokes.

Your picture has a lovely matting around the oval picture, and the frame is narrow and classy looking with white glossy paint.

"Both of you are beautiful pictures even though you look so different. However, you're not seeing the beauty in the other person's picture. In fact, you keep trying to repaint the picture to make it look more like your own. This week I'd like you to look for the beauty that is a part of each of your pictures, just the way you are. And let's get back together next week and talk about it."

What a difference a week can make. Using that one word picture communicated volumes to this couple. Instead of trying to change each other into their own image, they actually began looking at the beauty in each other's life and rediscovered the attraction that had drawn them together in the first place. Instead of dishonoring each other in anger, they began to be more patient with each other by recognizing the other person's uniqueness.

Whether we are dealing with defensive people, or those who battle with insecurity, using a word picture can help us get around their defenses and help us attach high value to them.

THE FOURTH KEY: WORD PICTURES POINT OUT A PERSON'S POTENTIAL

A fourth reason for using word pictures is to illustrate the undeveloped traits of a person. Jesus did this in changing Simon's name to Peter (literally "rock" in Greek). Peter certainly didn't act like a rock of strength and stability when he tried to talk Jesus out of going to the cross, when he went to sleep in the garden, or when he denied Jesus three times. But Jesus knew Peter's heart; and after the Resurrection, Peter became the rock he was pictured to be. In a modern-day instance, we saw this happen with a young lady in our church.

Several years ago, this young woman's husband divorced her to pursue an immoral relationship. Left with two young children under three, and no marketable skills or experience in the work force, she faced one struggle after another. Today, six years later, she has a good job that allows her time to spend with her children and still to provide for their basic financial needs. When we asked her what was the greatest source of help to her during those first, difficult years, she said:

"The Lord was certainly the greatest source of help to us when Jack first left; but from a human perspective, I would have to point to my father. Every time I wanted to quit school or just give up, he would say to me, 'You'll make it, Jenny. You're my rock of Gibraltar. I know you'll make it.' I didn't feel like a rock at the time. My whole world seemed to be caving in. But it helped me so much to know that he pictured me this way. It gave me the hope that maybe I could make it." We can give this same hope to others when we use a word picture to describe their abilities, abilities they might not acknowledge or even be aware of.

To review, we have discovered four keys to using word pictures in communicating words of high value:

- Use an everyday object.
- Match the emotional meaning of the trait you are praising with the object you've picked.
- Word pictures unravel our defenses.
- Word pictures can point out a person's potential.

A well-known saying tells us that one picture is worth a thousand words. When we link a word picture with a message of high value, we multiply our message a thousand times.

In the next chapter, we will look at the fourth major element of the blessing. Closely tied with words of high value is a message of a special future in store for the person being blessed.

—6—

The Fourth Element of the Blessing: Picturing a Special Future

—❧—

"*H*ow could anyone as dumb and ugly as you have such a good-looking child?" Mark's mother was grinning as she cuddled her grandson in her arms. To most observers, her words might have been brushed aside as a bad joke; but almost instantly, they brought tears to Mark's eyes.

"Stop it!" Mark said emphatically. "That's all I've ever heard from you. It's taken me years to believe I'm not ugly and dumb. Why do you think I haven't been home in so long? I don't ever want you to call me dumb again."

Mark's mother sat in stunned silence. Tears came to her eyes. After all, she really had meant her words as a joke. But for the first time, one of her children had had the courage to confront her. For years, without realizing the impact of her words, this mother had constantly kidded her children about being stupid, fat, or ugly. After all, she had been kidded unmercifully by *her* mother when she was growing up. . . .

What Kind of Future Do Our Words Picture?

When it comes to predictions about their future, children are literalists—particularly when they hear predictions from their parents, the most important people from an earthly perspective, in their lives. For this reason, communicating a special future to a child is such an important part of giving the blessing. When a person feels in his or her heart that the future is hopeful and something to look forward to, it can greatly affect his or her attitude on life. In this way we are providing our children, spouse, or friends with a clear light for their path in life.

Have you ever been camping in the woods on a dark night? If you have, you probably remember what it's like to walk away from your campfire into the night. In only a few steps, darkness can seem to swallow you up. Turning around and walking back toward the fire is a great deal more reassuring than groping around in the dark.

Words that picture a special future act like a campfire on a dark night. They can draw a person toward the warmth of genuine concern and fulfilled potential. Instead of leaving a child to head into a dark unknown, they can illuminate a pathway lined with hope and purpose.

Children begin to take steps down the positive pathway pictured for them when they hear words like these: "God has given you such a sensitive heart. I wouldn't be surprised if you end up helping a great many people when you grow older," or "You are such a good helper. When you grow up and marry someday, you're going to be such a help to your wife (or husband) and family." On the other hand, just the opposite is true as well.

If children hear only words that predict relationship problems or personal inadequacies, they can turn and travel down a hurtful path that has been pictured for them. This can happen if they hear statements like: "You'd better hope you can find someone who can take care of you when you're older. You're so irresponsible you'll never be able to do anything for yourself," or "Why bother to study so much? You'll just get married and drop out of school anyway." Let's look back at Mark's family to see how this happened in his home.

Over the years, Mark's mother had repeatedly given her children a negative picture of their future. "Nobody's going to want to date a fat mess like you!" she would say with a resounding laugh (and her daughter would ache inside). "You might as well drop geometry now; that's for smart kids," she would remark (and her youngest son would throw down his pencil and quit trying to understand the math problem in front of him, hating himself for giving up).

These were just playful words from the mother's perspective. Unfortunately, for her children, these words robbed them of an important part of the blessing, the critical need every child has to have a special future pictured for him or her.

In Mark's family, facing the future as dumb, ugly, or unappealing—even if such words were spoken in jest—eroded each child's self-confidence. The youngest son dropped out of high school after flunking his junior year. After all, he "never was intelligent" anyway. Mark's older sister neglected her appearance so much that no boys were interested in dating her. After all, she knew she was "ugly" anyway.

Mark had taken just the opposite approach to the negative future pictured for him. He became the family "overachiever." His entire lifestyle bordered on extreme workaholism in his need to be successful—all in an attempt to try to prove to his mother that her predictions were wrong.

If you add up the incredible costs extracted from the children in this family, you can see how devastating picturing a negative future can be. You can also see why the blessing in the Scriptures puts such a high priority on providing a special future for each child.

Picturing a Special Future in Patriarchal Homes

In the Old Testament, the fourth element of the blessing pictured a special future for children. We can see this by looking at the words Isaac spoke to Jacob.

"Therefore may God give you
Of the dew of heaven
Of the fatness of the earth,
And plenty of grain and wine.
Let peoples serve you
And nations bow down to you.
Be master over your brethren,
And let your mother's sons bow down to you.
Cursed be everyone who curses you,
And blessed be those who bless you!" (Gen. 27:28–29).

When Isaac spoke these words, much of his son's blessing lay in the future. Jacob was not swamped with people
wanting to bow down to him, and he had no land or
flocks of his own that God could bless. Yet the picture of
a fulfilling future was a powerful gift. The picture gave
him the security of knowing he had something to look
forward to.

One generation later, Jacob's son, Judah, received a
blessing that pictured a special future for him. Jacob
blessed him with these words: "Judah, you are he whom
your brothers shall praise; / Your hand shall be on the
neck of your enemies; / Your father's children shall bow
down before you" (Gen. 49:8).

Like father, like son—Jacob passed down this part of
the blessing. This blessing pictured a special future that
would take years to become reality, but offered Judah a
special hope as each year unfolded.

As we noted in Chapter Two, these patriarchs' words
had a prophetic nature that is not a part of the blessing
today. We as parents cannot predict our children's future with biblical accuracy, but we can provide them
with the hope and direction that is part of picturing
meaningful goals. Our children can begin to live up to
these goals and so will gain added security in an insecure world, the kind of personal goals still pictured in
many Jewish homes.

In orthodox Jewish homes and services, the wish for a
special future for each child is constantly present. At the
synagogue, the rabbi often says to young boys:

> May this little child grow to manhood. Even as he has en-
> tered into the Covenant, so may he enter into the study of
> Torah, into the wedding-canopy and into a life of good
> deeds.[1]

In orthodox Jewish homes, blessing children is also in-
terlaced with words that picture a special future. We saw
this blessing with a special future in a Jewish home we
were invited to visit one Thanksgiving. By the time we
arrived, almost forty people were preparing or waiting
patiently for a scrumptuous dinner. With the grandparents, parents, and their children, three generations
had assembled for this special occasion.

When the meal was prepared and before it could be
served, the patriarch of the family (the grandfather in
this case) gathered all the family together. He had all the
men and their sons stand on one side of the living room,
and all the women and their daughters stand on the
other side. He then went around, placing his hands on
the head of every person in the room saying to each man,
"May God richly bless you, and may He make thee as
Ephraim and Manasseh" and to each woman, "May God
richly bless you, and may you grow to be like Rebekah
and Sarah."

From the oldest child, to the youngest grandchild, this
time of blessing pictured a special future for each person
in the room. Far from being a meaningless ritual, the
blessing provided everyone with a warm wish for a fulfilling life in the years to come.

Bringing Out the Best in Those We Bless

Picturing a special future for a child, spouse, or friend
can help bring out the best in their lives. It gives them a
positive direction to strive toward and surrounds them
with hope. We can see this very thing in our relationship
with the Lord. Listen to the beautiful way in which the
prophet Jeremiah assures us of the special future we
have in our relationship with the Lord: "For I know the

thoughts that I think toward you, says the LORD, thoughts
of peace and not of evil, to give you a future and a hope"
(29:11).

Jesus also went to great lengths to assure His insecure
disciples that they had a special future with Him. During
their last Passover meal together, Jesus made sure they
knew their future together would not end at His death.
In John 14:2–3 we read:

> "In my Father's house are many mansions; if it were not
> so, I would have told you. I go to prepare a place for you.
> And if I go and prepare a place for you, I will come again
> and receive you to Myself; that where I am, there you may
> be also."

Time and time again, God gives us a picture of our special future with Him in His Word. However, His written
Word is not the only way God communicates this message to us. Scattered throughout nature are a number of
physical pictures of spiritual truths, pictures that illustrate the importance of providing a special future for the
ones we love.

Anyone who has ever watched a caterpillar emerge
from its cocoon as a butterfly has seen such a picture.
The caterpillar is probably not on anyone's list of the
world's "ten most beautiful creatures." Yet a caterpillar
has the potential to be transformed into a list-topping,
beautiful butterfly. What does this have to do with the
blessing? Words that picture a special future for a child,
spouse, or friend can act as agents of transformation in
their lives.

Words really do have that kind of transforming power.
The apostle Paul certainly thought so.

The actual term for the transformation of a caterpillar
to a butterfly is the Greek word *metamorphosis*. Paul
used this same Greek word in the book of Romans, which
we translate as "transformed." In writing to the church
in Rome, Paul was aware that the world had tremendous
power to squeeze and mold these saints into a godless
image. To counter this, he tells these young believers to
"be transformed by the renewing of your mind, that you

may prove what is that good and acceptable and perfect will of God" (Rom. 12:2).

What does it mean to be "transformed by the renewing of your mind"? One excellent New Testament commentator explains the concept this way: "Since men are transformed by the action of the mind, transformed by what they think, how important to have the organ of thought renewed!"[2] In other words, godly thoughts and thinking patterns have the ability to transform us into godly men or women, rather than leaving us to be squeezed into the imperfect mold of the world. Let's see how this works with regard to the blessing.

Children are filled with the potential to be all God intended them to be. It is as if the Lord places them on our doorstep one day, and we as parents are left as stewards of their abilities. During the years we have children in our home, the words we speak to them can wrap themselves around them like a cocoon. What we say shapes and develops their thoughts and thinking patterns. Loving words that picture a special future help children change and develop in a positive way. In the previous chapter we saw how this picture of the future helped Diane.

In spite of her physical handicap, Diane's parents provided emotional support and words of a special future that lay before her. When she "emerged from the cocoon" of her parents' home and went off into the world, her love for the Lord and other people shone as brightly as the colors on a Monarch butterfly's wings.

In other homes, the words that wrap around developing children actually restrict growth and positive change, rather than promote it. This restriction was true in Barry's home.

"You're a bum. You'll always be a bum." Barry's father said these words to him on his way to his college graduation—a ceremony his father did not even attend. This was not the first time, nor the last, that Barry would hear these words. In fact, up until his father's death, they were the only comments Barry received about his future.

When we saw Barry in counseling, he had just lost an important position in a major insurance company. At first glance, it seemed hard to believe. Barry was extremely intelligent and gifted. He was an eloquent speaker and had that charisma that marks many successful businessmen. However, in less than a year after he had been given an important position in this company he had self-destructed.

Barry demonstrated all the motivation in the world in the way he worked to land his job; but all that motivation seemed to evaporate once he was hired. He became irresponsible in handling projects and people, and within six months he was looking for work.

What was it that acted like an anchor in holding Barry back from reaching his God-given potential? Three words: "You're a bum." Repeated over and over in Barry's mind (even eight years after his father's death), they wrapped themselves around him like a cocoon; and he emerged an insecure, irresponsible, and defeated man. Barry was searching for the acceptance found in the blessing he missed.

A law of physics says that water cannot rise above its source. A similar principle could be applied to Barry and many people like him. If a parent pictures for a child that his or her value in life is low, that child will find it difficult to rise above these words. In one insightful study of fathers and their daughters, it was found that these women's achievements in life were directly related to the level of their father's acceptance of them.[3] Those who truly desire to give their children the blessing will provide the room for these boys and girls to grow by encouraging their potential and by picturing a special future for them.

Let's look at another important picture in nature that mirrors what happens when we bless our children with words of a special future. This picture is of something that happens in every cell in our body.[4]

Imagine a typical cell in our body by thinking of a circle. Attached to the outside of this circle are a number of receptor points. We could picture these receptor points as little squares that almost look like gears on a wheel. To make things easier for us to understand, let's picture these receptor sites as little square people.

Floating around near the cell are "Harry" hormone and "Ethyl" enzyme. They would each love to shake hands with (or activate) these little receptor sites. In fact a great number of these hormones and enzymes could grasp hold of a receptor site, but some have a special ability to stimulate a cell's activity. We can picture this special ability as someone coming up to you and shaking your hand up and down so vigorously that your whole body shakes! This stimulation is called "positive cooperativity"; and not only does this one receptor site get to shaking (and working harder as a result), but all the other receptor sites around it get to shaking and working harder as well!

Other hormones and enzymes act in a negative way when they "shake hands" with a receptor site (called "negative cooperativity"). Have you ever had your hand squeezed so hard that you almost crumpled over in pain? That's the kind of thing that happens when these hormones and enzymes grab hold of a receptor site. In fact, not only does this one receptor site shut down and stop working because its "hand" is being squeezed, but all the receptor sites around it stop too.

Words that picture a special future for a child act like positive hormones that attach themselves to a child. In fact, they stimulate all kinds of positive feelings and decisions within a child that can help him or her grow and develop. With words of a special future, a child can begin to work on a particular talent, have the confidence to try out for a school office, or even share his or her faith with other children. But just like the negative hormones that shut down cell activity, a critical, negative picture of the future can pinch off healthy growth in a child. Emotional, physical, and even spiritual growth in a child can be stunted because of the stifling effect of a negative picture of the future.

Putting Words of a Special Future into Practice

No more pictures of butterflies or cells shaking hands! Now we *know* how important it is to provide our children with words that point out a special future for them. However, to make sure we not only understand this principle, but also know how to apply it in our homes, let's look at two practical ways to make sure our message gets across to those we want to bless. We'll begin by taking two steps back to make sure our past actions do not undermine our words about the future.

CONSISTENCY IN THE PAST

Inconsistency in the past can make a person unwilling to believe our words in the present. If we are serious about offering a message of a special future to our children, we need to follow the example the Lord sets. His consistency in the past acts like a solid footing on which words of a special future can stand.

Throughout the Scriptures, the basis for believing God's word in the future lies in His consistency in fulfilling His word in the past. In Psalm 105:5 we read: "Remember His marvelous works which He has done, His wonders, and the judgments of His mouth." And in Psalm 33:9 the psalmist wrote: "He spoke, and it was done; He commanded, and it stood fast."

Because God has been reliable in the past, His words of a special future for us in the present have credence. The same principle is true in our desire to provide a special future for those we wish to bless. Our credibility in the past will directly affect how our words are received in the present. Just as it did for Ted.

Ted was a sales manager for a national marketing chain. His job responsibilities meant that he was in town one week and out the next. In an average year (adding in an occasional "back to back" trip and sales conferences and subtracting major holidays), Ted was gone thirty-one weeks a year. His schedule ate away at the credibility of his words that his children had a special future.

Ted had two young children at home, and they loved their daddy dearly. All week they would besiege their mother with the question, "Is Daddy coming home today?" When Daddy finally did come home, he was so tired from "jet-lag" and his demanding schedule that he didn't have the energy to spend meaningful time with the children.

Ted did a good job of "picturing" a special future for his children. The only problem was that he never followed through on his word. He had noticed his daughter's deep love for animals, and he would say, "Samantha, we're going to get a horse for you so you can ride it and take care of it. You might even become a veterinarian someday." His son was very athletic for his age, and he would say to him, "Bobby, you're pro shortstop material. Just give me a little time to rest up, and we'll go down to the park and I'll hit you some grounders." However, a few days would pass and then it was time for Ted to go back on the road. Somehow there was never enough time to settle all the details on what kind of pony Sam should get and where they would stable it; nor a free afternoon to hit grounders to Bobby, a potential shortstop.

After nine years of being on the road, Ted finally realized that he needed to greatly reduce his traveling schedule if he was ever going to build a secure marriage and family life.

Ted even took a cut in pay to move to a position in the company where he could stay at home. One of the first things he did was to surprise his daughter with a new pony—only now, nine years later, Samantha wasn't interested in horses anymore. Neither was Bobby interested in going with his father to a pro baseball game. His children had listened to the empty promise of a special future for them so long that Ted's words carried as much weight as the air used to speak them. They had their friends, their relationship with their mother, a new set of interests, and a deep-set impression that any future they had would not include their father being involved in it.

This story has a happy ending, however. Ted truly

loved his wife and children, and he persevered in trying to regain lost ground with his family. As the weeks turned into months, Ted was beginning to build up a track record of honored commitments. It took nearly two years, but Ted finally built up a "past" with his children that assured them he really did want the best for their future. Interestingly, Samantha even began to rekindle an interest in animals, and Bobby dug his baseball glove out of the bottom of the closet.

Perhaps your past has been anything but consistent with those you want to bless. Today really *is* the first day of the rest of your life. And you can begin to build the kind of "past" that words of a special future need to rest on by honoring commitments to your children today. Remember, there is no such thing as inconsistent "quality" time that makes up for consistency in our relationships. We need to have a track record of daily decisions that demonstrate our commitment to our children, our spouse, or anyone we would bless. Only then will our words of a special future really find their mark.

COMMITMENT IN THE PRESENT

As we mentioned above, if our words of a special future are to take hold and grow, we need to demonstrate commitment in the present. This idea of commitment is so important, we will spend the entire next chapter looking at it. Commitment is the fifth element of the blessing. However, one aspect of a present commitment applies directly to our look at picturing a special future. That aspect is the degree of certainty our children have in whether we will be around long enough to see our predictions come to pass. I (Gary) saw this clearly one night at the dinner table in something my grade-school daughter said.

We were all sitting around the table, enjoying a meal my wife, Norma, had prepared. We were all talking about our day and having a nice conversation, when out of the blue Kari turned to her mother and said, "Mom, do you think you'll ever divorce Dad?" Everyone got quiet the moment she asked her question, and Norma nearly choked on her dinner. "Kari!" she said in shock, "You know that I would never divorce your dad." Then stopping to think about it a little more, Norma added with a twinkle in her eye, "Murder maybe, but never divorce!"

After we stopped laughing, we found out why Kari had asked her question. We were only two months into the school year, and already the parents of two of her class-mates had gotten a divorce. What Kari was asking that night was the same thing every child asks (whether out loud to parents or in the silence of his or her heart) about his parents: "Will you be here in the future as I grow up, or will one of you leave me?"

Recently, I (John) counseled a couple where the husband and wife were constantly fighting. I had asked the entire family to come in to try to get a better picture of what was happening between the couple. That meant that I had an eleven-year-old boy and a six-year-old girl join us for our counseling session. I began the session by addressing my first question to this six-year-old young lady (children are *soooooo* honest, even when their parents hesitate to be too specific).

"What bothers you the most about your parents' argu-ing?" I asked. What was causing her the greatest pain and insecurity wasn't their loud voices or even what they said. What concerned her most was the surprising an-swer she gave me. "Every time my Daddy gets mad at my Mom, he takes off his wedding ring and throws it away."

Children are incredibly perceptive, and this little girl was no exception. While her father said it was "no big deal," his habit of pulling his wedding ring off his finger and throwing it somewhere in the house sent out a mes-sage loud and clear. Every time he "threw away" his wedding ring, this little girl saw her future with her par-ents (the greatest source of security a child has) go sail-ing right along with it.

Words of a special future for a child can dissolve into ashes when a husband or wife walks out on a relation-

ship. In a later chapter, we will see just how difficult it is
for some children to feel blessed who have lost a parent
due to divorce or death (and also how a single parent can
help correct this). For those of you who are married, an
important part of picturing a special future for your children is keeping your present commitment to your spouse
strong and intact.

A Guiding Light to Follow

Thankfully, many people realize the importance of
providing their children, spouse, or friends with a picture of a special future. These people know how to use
words of blessing to help mold, shape, and guide others
into the full potential God has in store for them. Even
when that person was labeled a "slow learner" like
Marcia.

Marcia struggled throughout her years in school. If it
took her classmates a half hour to do an assignment, you
can bet Marcia would only be halfway through the same
project an hour later. Her parents even received the dis-
turbing news from her teacher that she was being placed
in the "slow learners" group. However even this news
did not discourage Marcia's parents from picturing a
special future for her. While they knew she was struggling in school, they also knew that their daughter had
many positive characteristics.

Rather than pushing Marcia to "hurry up" or read
faster, her parents would praise her for being methodical
and for staying with an assignment until she finished it.
They also noticed that Marcia had an obvious gift for verbally encouraging her younger sisters and the neighbor
children and for explaining things to them in a way they
could understand. They began to encourage her to use
these talents by letting her help them teach the young
children in Sunday school and use her gifts in serving
these little ones.

After Sunday school one morning, Marcia announced
to her parents that she wanted to be a teacher when she

grew up. Her comments could have been met with a chuckle, a "What'll you want to be next week," or even the pious words, "Now Marcia, let's be realistic" (particularly when the quarter's grades had just come out and Marcia was still at the bottom of her class). However, Marcia's parents looked beyond her sagging test scores and saw the God-given talents Marcia had.

Instead of laughing at her, they pointed out these gifts and encouraged her. They said that if she was willing to stay with it, one day she could become a teacher. This picture is of a future few "slow learners" would ever dream of painting for themselves or ever hear pictured for them by their parents.

Marcia struggled through every year of school. Her parents had to provide and pay for tutors in grade school and special reading classes in high school. When Marcia decided to go to college, it took her six and a half years to graduate from a four-year program because she could not handle taking a full load of classes. Nonetheless, on a beautiful Saturday afternoon in May, Marcia graduated from college with an elementary education teaching degree.

While graduation day meant that many of her classmates were just beginning to look for a job, Marcia already had one. She had done such a magnificent job of student-teaching at an elementary school in a fine school district that the principal had asked her to return the next year and take over a first grade teaching position.

Actually, three people deserved to be honored that graduation day. Marcia certainly deserved a great deal of credit for plodding forward day by day to reach her goal of being an elementary school teacher. Yet her parents also deserved high praise for encouraging her to reach her dream. Even more, they deserved acclaim for encouraging their daughter's dream by picturing a special future for her—even when years worth of grade school report cards had branded Marcia a "slow learner."

Are you providing your children, spouse, or intimate friends with a blessing that pictures a special future for

them? Did your parents take the time and effort to provide you with the hope of a bright tomorrow as you grew
up? Wherever the blessing is given or received words
that picture a special future are always spoken, words
that represent the fourth element of the blessing.

— 7 —

The Fifth Element of the Blessing: An Active Commitment

---

*M*ost children have at least one subject in school that they particularly dread. Whether it is history, English, geography, or in my (Gary's) case, geometry, that course represents the worst hour of their school day.

Mathematics was always the subject I dreaded the most. In grade school it was my poorest subject, and that continued to be true during my first two years of high school. In fact, when I had to repeat geometry my senior year I was sure after only a month that I was going to flunk the course. One reason I had such a difficult time getting into the subject was because my teacher felt sure I was going to flunk the course. My only solace was the fact that more than half the class was flunking with me. Our teacher would constantly remind us of this fact by arranging our chairs according to our current grade. Those of us who were failing lined the back wall.

One Monday morning when we dragged ourselves into the classroom all that changed. Sitting behind the teacher's desk was a substitute teacher. That was good news in itself! Then when we found out that our regular teacher had been reassigned to a different district, we felt like the people in Paris during World War II who had just been liberated! The only problem that remained was that half of us were still failing the course. I was particularly discouraged. A new teacher might bring some relief, I reasoned, but I still felt I was below average when it came to mathematics.

Something that teacher said that morning literally changed my life. In fact, it motivated me so much that I ended up minoring in mathematics in college! While I didn't realize it at the time, he actually blessed me and the other students in the class. He did this by providing us with a clear picture of an active commitment—the fifth element of the blessing.

Standing before the class that morning, our new teacher told us, "If anyone fails this class, then I have failed." He made a commitment that morning to do whatever it took to see that we all passed the course. He pledged himself to see that we learned and enjoyed the subject to the best of our abilities. Whether that meant his staying after school to tutor us or even coming in for a special session on the weekend, he dedicated himself to seeing that each of us made it through the course. Nearly every Saturday morning he would help several of us with our homework, and then he played a little volleyball with us for fun.

Imagine the turnaround that took place in that class. Where once we dreaded coming, now it became something we looked forward to. Even better was what happened at the end of the school year. When our teacher posted our grades the last day of class, we all passed! I even received my first *A* in math! You should have seen it. We were all jumping around and hugging each other. All because one man committed himself to a struggling bunch of students.

In the school of life, children desperately need parents who will make that same type of active commitment to them. In the areas in which they are weak, they need to be encouraged and built up. They need to be hugged and verbally praised for their strengths. When they are hurting, their parents' arms need to be around them giving them assurance and helping them back on their feet. Undeveloped potential needs to be brought out into the open and developed—even if it takes our weekends. These actions and attitudes are a part of bestowing the blessing.

In the past four chapters we have looked at the first four elements of the blessing:

- Meaningful touch
- Spoken words
- Expressing high value
- Picturing a special future

These four elements are the building blocks of the blessing. But the mortar that holds them together is an active commitment—the fifth element of the blessing.

Two Ways to Express an Active Commitment

What do we mean by "active commitment," and why is it such an important part of the blessing? Commitment is important because as we have seen in earlier chapters, words of blessing alone are not enough. They need to be backed by the commitment of a person to see the blessing come to pass. This principle is what the apostle James wants us to understand in his letter. There we read:

> If a brother or sister is naked and destitute of daily food, and one of you says to them, "Depart in peace, be warmed and filled," but you do not give them the things which are needed for the body, what does it profit? (James 2:15–16).

To answer his question, such words are about as useful as a crooked politician's shouting promises on election eve. Children of all ages need the daily "food and clothing" of love and acceptance that the blessing can provide. Yet like the verse we have just read, mere words of blessing are not enough.

We need to take action if we are to give the blessing. If we "talk the talk" but then fail to put the elements of the blessing into practice in our home, we leave our children undernourished and ill-clothed in their need for love and acceptance.

In strong contrast to speaking empty words to our

loved ones is the blessing in the Scriptures. It pictures two ways we can make sure we have an active commitment to our children, spouse, or others. These steps begin by asking the Lord to be the one who confirms their blessing.

THE FIRST STEP: COMMIT THE PERSON
BEING BLESSED TO THE LORD

When you look at the blessing in the Old Testament, something that stands out is the way the patriarchs committed their children to the Lord. When Isaac blessed Jacob, we read: "May *God* give you of the dew of the heaven, / Of the fatness of the earth" (Gen. 27:28, italics added). Years later, when Jacob blessed his sons and grandchildren, he began by saying, "The *God* who has been my shepherd all my life to this day . . . bless these lads" (Gen. 48:15–16 NASB, italics added). One reason why they called on God to confirm their child's blessing was because they were sure of His commitment to them. We can see this clearly with Isaac and Jacob.

In Genesis 26, Isaac was facing real problems. Living in the desert, he knew that his most precious commodities were the wells he dug for fresh water. Twice Isaac had been driven from wells his father had dug. Finally, he had to dig a third well to provide water for his flocks and his family. As if to assure Isaac of his future in this land, we read: "And the Lord appeared to him the same night and said, 'I am the God of your father Abraham; do not fear, for I am with you. I will bless you, and multiply your descendants'" (Gen. 26:24, italics added).

Isaac had been driven away from two wells that rightfully belonged to him. Hearing his heavenly Father declare His commitment to him must have been like drinking cool refreshing water on a hot summer's day.

God echoed His words of commitment to Jacob at a difficult time in his life. Fleeing his brother Esau's anger, he stopped one night to sleep out in the desert. It was there that God spoke to him and said:

"I am the LORD God of Abraham your father and the God of Isaac. . . . Behold, I am with you and will keep you wherever you go, and will bring you back to this land; for I will not leave you until I have done what I have spoken to you" (Gen. 28:13–15).

Isaac and Jacob were sure of their relationship with God. A natural extension of that certainty was to ask the Lord to bless their children through them. This is something we frequently see in churches today.

This past Sunday, in churches all across the country, the pastor closed the service with the words, "May the Lord bless you, and keep you." By linking God's name to the blessing he spoke, the pastor was asking God Himself to be the one to confirm it with His power and might, the very thing Isaac and Jacob did with their children.

We also see this in a "children's dedication" at the church. Often the pastor will lay his hands on a child and bless the child, a picture of the desire the parents and the entire congregation have in asking God to bless this little one.

Wise parents will model this practice in bestowing the blessing on their children. When they say, "May the Lord bless you," they are first recognizing and acknowledging that any strength they have to bestow the blessing comes from an all-powerful God. Even the very breath of life they have to speak words of blessing comes from Him.

We are all prone to be inconsistent, and we stumble occasionally in providing the elements of the blessing for our children. In contrast, God remains changeless in His ability to give us strength to love our spouse and children in the way we should.

A second important reason to commit our children to the Lord when we bless them is that this teaches them that God is personally concerned with their life and welfare. Stressing the fact that the Lord is interested in their being blessed is like introducing them to someone who can be their best friend, a personal encourager they can draw close to throughout their lives.

When the Lord is brought into our words of blessing, it provides a sense of security for a child that we as frail humans cannot convey. We saw this in the way the children in one family reacted after the unexpected death of their father.

Karen and Nichole were still in grade school when their father died. He was only forty-one years old when he died of a massive heart attack. These children no longer had his arms to comfort them or his encouraging words to bless them. But they did have a certain knowledge that Papa was with the Lord, and that Jesus would confirm their blessing. Why such certainty? Because a wise father and mother had reassured them of this fact over and over. Listen to the words of his widow, Lisa, who also could draw comfort from her husband's words.

"Before Ray died, he used to gather us all together right before dinner. We would all get in a little circle, holding each other's hands. Then Papa would pray and thank the Lord for our day and for the food. He would end each prayer by squeezing my hand and saying, 'Lord Jesus, thank You that You are Karen's, and Nichole's, and Lisa's, and my shepherd. Thank You that You will never leave us or forsake us. Amen.' It's been rough this past year without Ray, but it has helped so much to be able to remind the children that Jesus is still their shepherd as well as their father's."

Children need the certainty and security that comes from our committing them and their blessing to the Lord. That does not mean that we do not participate in the blessing. Rather, it means that we recognize and acknowledge that only by God's strength and might will we ever be able to truly bless our children.

THE SECOND STEP: COMMIT OUR LIVES
TO THEIR BEST INTERESTS

How do we begin committing ourselves to our children's best interest? First, as we have noted throughout the book, it takes a commitment of our time, energy, and resources. However, Jacob observed another important principle in blessing his children. He recognized that every one of his children was unique.

In Genesis 48 and 49, Jacob (now called Israel) pronounced a blessing for each of his twelve sons and two of his grandchildren. After he had finished blessing each child, we read: "This is what their father [Jacob] said to them; when he blessed them. He blessed them, *every one*, with the blessing appropriate to him" (Gen. 49:28 NASB, italics added).

In Hebrew, the end of this verse reads, "He blessed them, every one with his own blessing." While the elements of the blessing might remain the same, how they are applied in blessing a child is an individual concern. One daughter might need a dozen "hugs and kisses" at night before going to bed, while her sister does well with two. One son might feel secure with hearing encouraging words only once, while his brother may need to hear "You can do it" over and over again in approaching the same activity.

Wise parents will realize that each child has his or her own unique set of needs. The book of Proverbs shows us this.

Most of us are familiar with the verse, "Train up a child in the way in which he should go, and when he is old he will not depart from it" (Prov. 22:6). However, another helpful way to view this verse would be to translate it, "Train up a child according to his bent. . . ."[1] In training (or blessing) a child, we need to take a personal interest in each child. The better we know our children and their unique set of needs, the better we will be able to give them their own unique blessing.

Please pay close attention to this next statement: Physical proximity does not equal personal knowledge. We can spend years under the same roof with our spouse and children and still be intimate strangers. Many people feel as though they "know" another person's interests and opinions because they took an active interest in their lives in the past. However, people's thoughts, dreams, and desires can change over the years. Doctors tell us that every cell in our body wears out and is re-placed by new cells within a few years. We are constantly changing physically and emotionally.

In our homes, we can be people who are close in terms of proximity to each other, but far away in terms of un-derstanding the other person's real desires, needs, goals, hopes, and fears. However, we can combat this by taking the time to understand the unique aspects of those we wish to bless.

Blessing our children involves understanding their unique bent. In addition, it means being willing to do what is best for that person—even if it means having to correct them when they are wrong.

Blessing Our Children Also Involves Disciplining Them

We want to show you a second way we can actively commit ourselves to our children's best interest. While it may seem the very opposite of "blessing" another per-son, in actuality we bless our children by providing them with appropriate discipline. We see this when we look back at the individual blessings Jacob gave to each of his children.

Genesis 49 records a blessing for each son. We are told this very clearly in verse 28, "He [Jacob] blessed them, every one with the blessing appropriate to him" (NASB). However, at first glance the blessing that Reuben, the oldest son, received looks more like a curse than a bless-ing. However, Jacob dealt with each son individually, and in Reuben's case his blessing included discipline as well as praise:

> "Reuben, you are my firstborn,
>   My might and the beginning of my strength,
>   The excellency of dignity and the excellency of power.
>   Unstable as water, you shall not excel,
>   Because you went up to your father's bed;
>   Then you defiled it" (Gen. 49:3–4).

If we look closely at these verses, Jacob balances words of praise with words of correction. Reuben had several positive qualities his father praised (his might, strength, dignity, and power). However he also had a glaring lack of discipline in his life. His unbridled passions led him to the bed of one of his father's concubines. As a result he now was being disciplined for his actions.

It should not surprise us that blessing and discipline go hand in hand. If we genuinely love someone, we will not allow him or her to stray into sin or be hurt in some way without trying to correct our loved one. This lesson the writer of Hebrews explains to us when he says, "My son, do not regard lightly the discipline of the Lord . . . for those whom the Lord loves He disciplines" (Heb. 12:5–6 NASB).

God actively deals with us as children rather than merely ignoring our wrong behavior. With other people's children, many earthly parents couldn't care less about their actions. However, like a loving parent with a highly valued child, God does care about our behavior.

Our sons' and daughters' actions will also concern us if we are going to be a person who truly blesses them. We should not shy away from including loving discipline when it is appropriate and in their best interest.[2]

Initially, disciplining another person can seem painful for both parties. Yet being willing to take that risk can help bring out the best in that person's life by training that person and guiding him or her to a place of peace and righteousness (Heb. 12:11). Discipline is an important way of actively committing ourselves to a person's best interest.

We have already looked at two ways in which we can demonstrate an active commitment in blessing others. We can commit them to the Lord and we can seek their best interest. A third way we can demonstrate an active commitment to them is to become a student of those we wish to bless. This is something I (John) have seen modeled before me all my life.

THIRD STEP: BECOME A STUDENT
OF THOSE WE WISH TO BLESS

Nestled away in a modest condominium in southern Arizona lives a sixty-four-year-old woman. Seven major operations due to rheumatoid arthritis have slowed her down a bit; but she is still busy, active, and lots of fun to visit.

If you were to drop in on her some day, you would see something in her home that pictures what it means to be a "student of your children." While it might not catch your eye right off, whenever I walk into my mother's home, it flashes at me like a neon light. What is it? It is a nondescript-looking bookshelf, but it carries special meaning for my two brothers and me.

One rack of the bookshelf is filled with theology and psychology books, and a second is filled with medical journals and books on genetics. The third shelf seems even more out of place for a sixty-four-year-old, arthritic woman. Lining this shelf are past issues of *Heavy Equipment Digest* and "How to" books on driving heavy equipment.

These seemingly unrelated books and magazines might lead a person to think this woman is an "eccentric" who reads anything, or perhaps even has a touch of schizophrenia that causes her to jump from one topic to the next. Neither of these explanations would be close to the truth. This collection is actually a beautiful picture of the active commitment our mother has made in giving us the blessing.

Over the years, in my studies in seminary and in my doctoral program, my mother has asked for and read numerous popular books and textbooks on theology and psychology. They are in her bookcase because she has taken an interest in my interests.

My twin brother, Jeff, is a medical doctor who specializes in genetic research in the battle against cancer. To try to understand his field of interest and to be able to converse with him about it, she has read (or tried to read) medical and genetics books. At the age of sixty, she even enrolled in a beginning genetics class at a local university!

To be truthful, she ended up dropping the course after failing the first two major exams. However, sitting proudly on the shelf with other highly technical books is the slightly worn textbook she struggled to understand. Each book is a trophy of her willingness to learn and her desire to communicate with my brother in his areas of interest.

What about the magazines and books on operating road construction equipment? My older brother, Joe, is now Director for Dealer Support for a national company; but for several years he excelled as a heavy equipment operator. Because my mother was also interested in what this son was involved in, she subscribed to *Heavy Equipment Digest* just so she would know about the latest bulldozer or earth mover.

This magazine does not get many subscription requests from sixty-four-year-old, grey-haired, arthritic women—but they did from this one. All because she made a commitment to become a student of each son and of his individual interests.

FIRST STEPS TOWARD BECOMING A STUDENT OF YOUR CHILDREN

We would like to give you some practical help in how you can become a student of your children, spouse, or others. One thing that can greatly help is to be lovingly persistent in communicating with them. I (Gary) learned this lesson from my oldest son, Greg, when we were both on a television talk show.

We were on a talk show discussing my parenting book, *The Key to Your Child's Heart*. Because my children actually helped me write the book, I had brought Greg on the show with me to share his perspective on parent/child communication. I learned a great deal about my son, and about children in general, by listening to one of his answers to a question.

The show's host asked Greg what one thing he would urge parents to do to communicate with their children. Without hesitation Greg said, "Don't believe it when your son or daughter tells you they 'Don't want to talk.' Sometimes I'll say that to my dad and mom when they ask me how I'm doing, but I don't mean it. I'm really hoping they will be persistent and help me talk about it."

Particularly if we have struggled in our relationships with our children or we haven't been close to them in the past we must be lovingly persistent in encouraging them to talk. That doesn't mean badgering them or trying to pry the words out of their mouths. We must consistently set up times with them when meaningful communication can develop.

In our parenting book, we talk about a second step toward becoming a student of those we wish to bless—the importance of sharing activities.[3] Not only do they draw us closer together, but sharing activities with our children offers tremendous opportunities to learn about our children.

My younger son, Mike, and I went hunting together recently. With deadlines to face in writing books and with a busy traveling schedule, I was not too thrilled about taking a week to walk up and down steep mountains. However, I knew it would be a tremendous time to spend with my son.

Sitting next to each other on the flight, walking in the woods, sitting by the campfire—these are the kinds of "unguarded" moments when meaningful conversation can take place. Without having to "manufacture" conversation, we ended up talking about some of his dreams, his girlfriend situation, and on and on. In some ways, I felt as though I had been re-introduced to my son.

"But I don't know what to ask them about themselves or how to get started!" For those parents who want to become a student of their children, but need some questions to get them started in conversation, here are several that you can begin to ask in those unguarded times at the hamburger place, at the ball game, or just taking a walk. Taking the initiative in asking questions can be a third important way to become a student of our children.

Do I Know the Following Things about My Children?

1. What do they most often daydream about?

2. When they think of their years as a young adult (twenty to thirty), what would they really enjoy doing?

3. Of all the people they have studied in the Bible, who is the person they would most like to be like, and why?

4. What do they believe God wants them to do for humankind?

5. What type of boyfriend or girlfriend are they most attracted to, and why?

6. What is the best part of their school day, and what is the worst?

Let's look a little closer at each of these.

These are just a few questions that can help us become a student of our children. We can and should ask our children many more to help us learn about them and so to value them for who they really are.

A fourth practical way to get started in becoming a student of those we wish to bless is to listen to them with our full attention. We actually bless our children by being emotionally present when they talk to us rather than by being preoccupied with something else.

Many of us at some time or another have carried on an entire conversation with our children while we were absorbed in the evening news or in reading the paper. "Uh, huh" and "That sounds good, Honey" uttered with our head in the newspaper does not communicate acceptance to our children; nor does it help us become a student of what they want to share.

One way to remind ourselves to actively listen to our children, spouse, or others is found in the book of Proverbs: "Bright eyes gladden the heart" (Prov. 15:30 NASB).

Most of us have had the experience of walking into a room and seeing somebody's eyes "light up" when he or she sees us. That sparkle in another person's eyes communicates to us that that person is really interested in us and in what we have to say. An interesting research study was done based on this very verse.

In this study, a number of college men were given ten pictures of college-aged women who were nearly equally attractive. Each student was then asked to rate the pictures from "most attractive" to "least attractive."

What these young men did not know was that five of the women had been given an eye-drop solution just before their picture was taken. This solution dilated the pupils in their eyes, the same thing that happens naturally when we are really glad to see someone! The results of the study were just as we might expect. The girls with "bright eyes" were chosen hands down as the five most attractive women in the pictures!

Do our eyes "light up" when we listen to those we wish to bless? Our children or our spouse will notice if they do or don't. We can decide to put down the newspaper or turn off the television to talk to our loved ones as we take an active interest in their interests. Active listening is an important part of communicating acceptance and blessing to our loved ones.

Those of us who are parents need to realize that our children are incredibly complicated people. So are our wives or husbands. If we would begin today to list all their wishes, opinions, goals, and dreams, it would take us a lifetime to complete the task. That is just the right amount of time needed to finish the course entitled, "Becoming a Student of Your Loved Ones," a class men and women will enroll in if they are serious about bestowing an appropriate blessing to each person in their life. All it takes to register is a decision to actively commit ourselves to others and a pair of "bright eyes."

A Key to Continued Commitment

Many of us have shelves of notebooks from various marriage or parenting seminars, and pages of notes from the pastor's sermons. Typically, we will get excited about a certain principle we have read or a tape we have listened to, and it can make a dramatic difference in our lives. However, let a few weeks go by, and that book or tape usually finds its way to a dusty bookshelf with the other inspirational material.

In teaching people about blessing their children, we have seen dramatic changes in their lives. For the first time many people have come to grips with whether they ever received the blessing themselves and with how well they are doing in providing it for their children. We hope you have already seen your parent's home and your own in a new and challenging light. Yet like any other call to commitment, that inner voice that encourages us to bless our children can be heard less and less as time wears on.

How can we establish a pattern of commitment that can make each element of the blessing a permanent resident in our homes? The best thing we know of is found in a single word—accountability.

For some reason we don't fully understand, genuine commitment to provide the blessing for our loved ones grows best in small groups. When three or four couples take the time, week by week, to go through a book or tape series together, lasting changes can take place.

Imagine someone asking us how we did in terms of providing meaningful touching for our spouse or children that week; what encouraging words we spoke that attached high value to a son or daughter; or even asking on a "one-to-ten" scale, how high was our commitment to bless our family this week?

Even better, imagine a place where you can admit your struggles and learn from other people's insights (and mistakes). Does this description sound challenging and inspiring? It can happen during Sunday school at your church or in your home on a weeknight. All it takes is the courage to ask honest questions and a loving spirit to share God's truth and your own personal insights. And you need one more thing: the nerve to pick up the phone and call three or four other couples.

Even if you are not part of a small group, you can stop right now and ask your spouse or a close friend how well you are doing in being a source of blessing to them. If your children are old enough, you can even ask them how they think you're doing in terms of giving them the blessing. Children will usually be honest with you, and you can learn valuable lessons from them—if you will take the time to talk and listen to them. On the next page we have included an evaluation sheet that you can photocopy and use with your children, with your spouse, or in a group to help you get started in the accountability process.

We know that asking questions, and even more, being willing to answer them, can be threatening to some people. Even so, small groups or one-on-one conversations are a tremendous way to evaluate where we are at the present. These meetings also give us an added incentive to work on an area we are struggling with. Left on our own, most of us will tend to forget or sidestep these important areas. Faithful friends can help us face things and help us grow as a result. Their love and emotional support can share our sorrow and double our joy.

Accountability can help train us in how we can become even better vessels of blessing for those we love. It can also give us an edge in developing continued commitment as we seek to bestow the blessing.

One Final Look at the Cost of Commitment

No doubt about it, commitment is costly. If you are serious about committing yourself to blessing those you love, expect to pay a price. Not in monetary terms necessarily. A spouse and even small children are far too wise to be bought off with presents for very long. Rather think in terms of the time, energy, and effort you will need to invest to see the blessing become a reality in their lives. Is the price worth it? The book of Proverbs certainly seems to show us that it is.

The final chapter of Proverbs describes a woman who

blesses her family in many ways. She is industrious and loving, has a positive outlook on the future, and is committed to her husband and children. Of equal impor-

---

Personal Evaluation Sheet

On a scale of 1-to-10, how well am I doing in bestowing the blessing on my loved ones? Circle your response.

1. Do I meaningfully touch them?

1   2   3   4   5   6   7   8   9   10

RARELY   FREQUENTLY

2. Do I verbally speak words of blessing?

1   2   3   4   5   6   7   8   9   10

SELDOM   OFTEN

3. Am I attaching "high value" to the people I'm blessing?

1   2   3   4   5   6   7   8   9   10

LOW VALUE   HIGH VALUE

4. Have I pictured a special future for their life?

1   2   3   4   5   6   7   8   9   10

SELDOM   OFTEN

5. Overall, my commitment level to fulfill my words of blessing is:

1   2   3   4   5   6   7   8   9   10

VERY LOW   VERY HIGH

tance are her words to her family that are filled with wisdom and kindness.

Did she just happen to be born this way? Certainly not. Each of these qualities was developed at a price. What is often skipped over when this passage is taught is how often this woman was up at dawn and how hard she worked to bless her family with her actions and words. She used the same kind of energy that gets parents out of bed on the weekend to take their children camping or that is needed to stay up late helping a husband or wife complete a project.

Was it really worth all that effort? It was for this woman. Read what her family has to say about her and her decision to make a genuine commitment to them: "Her children rise up and call her blessed; / Her husband also, and he praises her: / 'Many daughters have done well, / But you excel them all'" (Prov. 31:28–29).

It takes hard work, wrapped in the words "active commitment," to provide the blessing to another person. It takes time to meaningfully touch and hug our children when they come home from school or before they go to bed. It takes courage to put into a spoken message those words of love for our spouse that have been on the tip of our tongue. It takes wisdom and boldness to "bow our knees" to highly value those we love. It takes creativity to picture a future for them filled with hope and with God's best for their lives. But all this effort is worthwhile.

One day, perhaps years later, that blessing will return. Your children will rise up and bless you. What's more, your joy at seeing another person's life bloom and grow because you have been committed to their best is a blessing in itself. Just ask one couple who took the time early in their only son's life to provide him with the blessing. When he grew up, he would provide words of blessing to his parents—in a most unusual way.

"Bubs" Roussel was only seventeen on that infamous Sunday morning in 1941 when Pearl Harbor was bombed. Later that day, he told his father and mother the shocking news of the Japanese attack.

Not long after, Bubs was called into the Army and ended up serving in the Army Air Corps (now called the Air Force). After special training in communications in Kansas, he was assigned as a radio operator in a B-29 bomber. The youngest in his crew, Bubs and many young men like him had to grow up fast. In only a few months he was stationed on the island of Saipan in the western Pacific.

From this tiny island, B-29s were making bomber runs on Japan. The work was dangerous and deadly. On the morning of December 13, 1944, eighteen bombers soared out over the Pacific to make a bomb run on factories at Nagoya, Japan. Four of the planes that left Saipan that morning never returned. Bubs's plane was among them.

Official word came from the War Department saying their son had been killed in action. Family members of each of Bubs's crew received along with the telegram a small white flag, bordered with red and trimmed with blue and gold. The flag had one small gold star in the middle—the symbol of a son who has fallen in battle.

Bubs's parents received something else. Almost a month after his plane went down, they received a letter Bubs had placed on his pillow before his last mission.

> Dear Folks:
>   I have left this with instructions to send it on to you if anything happens to me. I send you my love and blessings. My life has been a full one. I have been loved like very few persons ever. I love you all with the best that is in me. It hasn't been hard for me, knowing you believe in me, trust me, and stand behind me in fair or foul. Knowing this has made me strong.[4]

Would our children be able to write a letter like this to us? They could in homes committed to being a source of blessing, homes like the one in which Bubs grew up. The words might be different, but the sentiment would be the same. Giving our children the blessing is like casting bread upon the waters. In years to come, they too will rise up and bless us.

Our prayer for every person who reads this book is

that you will become a person of blessing. The cost is genuine commitment, but the rewards can last a lifetime and beyond.

For five chapters we have looked at homes that bestow that blessing on children. Unfortunately, not all children receive a blessing they can give back to their parents. Let's look now at the homes we see most commonly in counseling that withhold the blessing—and the consequences on their children and later generations as a result.

—8—

Homes That Withhold the Blessing: Part 1

---

*F*ew people see themselves as struggling with missing out on their family's blessing, but people around them see it. Whether it is reflected in an underlying sense of insecurity, or, more blatantly obvious, in an angry, hostile spirit, we can hide very little from those who know us well.

As we have noted all along in looking at the blessing, living for years with our family leaves a profound mark on us. In most cases, this mark is a positive one, issuing from a family that deeply cares for us. Yet some have struggled in homes where the blessing was never given. Often, the parents who withhold the blessing lack the knowledge or skill to pass on the blessing. But some homes have serious problems that can deeply scar a man or woman. These homes can cause an individual to wear the mark of his or her family like the mark of shame God put on Cain.

Such people can spend years struggling to free themselves from their past and as a result are never free to enjoy a commitment relationship in the present. If hurtful patterns from the past are not broken, they are likely to repeat themselves in the next generation. Unfortunately, this is where the terrible truth found in Exodus 20:5 comes true, a home where "the iniquity of the fathers" is passed down to the third and fourth generations.

In a later chapter, we will look at how these hurtful patterns from the past can be broken. We will also discover God's spiritual family blessing that can provide healing to those living apart from their parents' blessing. However, in the next two chapters, we want to introduce you to the five most common homes we see in counseling that withhold the blessing.

We recognize that there may be more homes than these; but in counseling couples and individuals all over the country, these five patterns have continued to surface time and time again. We also want to share with you seven characteristics of those we see who have never come to grips with living apart from the blessing. These characteristics will help us identify and better understand someone who has grown up apart from the blessing.

Before we begin our tour of these homes and common characteristics, we want to make one thing clear. In no way do we want this chapter to become ammunition to dishonor a parent or to become an excuse to blame all present problems on the past. In fact, just the opposite is true. We hope that speaking truthfully and honestly about these homes and patterns will lead us to honor our parents (perhaps for the first time) and take responsibility for how we behave today.

Only when we can honestly look at our parents and our past are we ever truly free to "leave" them in a healthy way and "cleave" to others in present relationships (Gen. 2:24). If we are carrying around anger or resentment from the past, we are not free to "leave." Rather, we are chained to the past and are likely to repeat it.

In gaining a better understanding of these homes that withhold the blessing and the characteristics they produce, we may also find we better understand our parents' backgrounds. Our parents were greatly influenced by growing up with their parents, and that experience reflects on us. By looking at the type of home our parents grew up in, we can often find answers to difficult questions about our parents that may have plagued us for years.

Our aim in the pages that follow is to inspire compassion, not heap criticism on horrible parents. Most horrible parents are people who truly love their children (even if they do not know how to show it) and have tried their best with the information they had. Even with those who have not, we can still decide to value them and forgive them just as God, in Christ, has forgiven us. To reinforce this desire, we will share in the pages that follow the stories of people who have actually worked through having missed out on the blessing—by applying the information we will make available in a later chapter.

God's Word gives help and hope to deal with the lack of the family blessing, hope that doesn't come from dishonoring our parents or burying our heads in the sand and ignoring the past. Yet before we can look at a remedy, we need to understand the problems that exist. Only then can we be free to move forward in the present and to receive help not to repeat a painful past.

With this important caution in mind, let's look at the first home that commonly withholds the blessing. In our first example, one child is showered with the blessing and the other children are not.

The First Home: Facing a Flood or a Drought

In the springtime, the Seattle area is particularly beautiful, lush, and green. Almost every day, clouds will roll in and drench the land with refreshing rain showers. However, if you leave the city and travel only a few hours east, up and over the mountains that are set in from the coastline, you will see a far different scene. These mountains do such an effective job in halting the rains that very few clouds get past them. As a result, the land on the east side of the mountains is actually semi-arid.

We can see a picture of a similar phenomenon in many

homes today. One child, for what can be a number of reasons, will be drenched with lush showers of blessing from his or her parents. As a result, outwardly this child thrives and grows.

Unfortunately, sitting "just east" of him or her at the dinner table can be one or more siblings whose emotional lives are like parched ground. So few drops of blessing have fallen on the soil of their lives that emotional cracks begin to form. This very thing happened in one Old Testament patriarch's home.

We are already familiar with the patriarch Jacob and the fact that at the end of his life he gave each son a special blessing. However, the Scriptures paint real life, not Hollywood fiction; and the facts are that Jacob showered only one son with the blessing when his children were young. We read about this in Genesis 37:3–4:

> Now Israel loved Joseph more than all his children, because he was the son of his old age. Also he made him a tunic of many colors. But when his brothers saw that their father loved him more than all his brothers, they hated him and could not speak peaceably to him (Gen. 37:3–4).

That beautiful tunic may have spelled special acceptance to one son, but it brought out hatred from eleven brothers. Each one knew at that time that he was living apart from the blessing. This anger reached such proportions that Joseph's brothers came close to putting him to death (Gen. 37:18–22).

Anger, resentment, and insecurity are often emotions that children carry who grow up without the blessing. Particularly when that blessing was so close, yet so far away. Like a thirsty man looking at rain falling at a distance, discouragement and depression can well up inside a child who is left out of the blessing. In such people's lives, emotional cracks and pain can result in persistent anger or resentment.

We normally think that only Joseph's brothers, or those like them, face all the problems in this type of home; but that is far from the truth. Both the children who miss out on the blessing and the one being showered with it can experience significant problems. We have seen this regularly in the one child who gained the blessing in a family but who feels guilty and defensive about receiving it.

Pro athletes commonly have this feeling. Often, because of their outstanding physical abilities, they are singled out for special praise far beyond any brother or sister. We talked to one athlete who feels this extra attention was a curse, not a blessing! He desperately wanted to have a close relationship with his brothers, but his parents' excessive attention to him kept his brothers at arm's length and left him aching with loneliness and feeling rejected inside.

Please don't misunderstand. Each child needs to be singled out sometimes for special praise or recognition. But if the elements of the blessing fall exclusively on one child, serious problems can develop for each child in the family. Just ask Joyce about her brother Jim.

Joyce was not merely showered with the blessing from her father, she was flooded with it! Her father paid so much attention to her that he rarely spoke words of blessing to her mother and her older brother, Jim.

Joyce and Jim's parents had struggled in their marriage for some time. In fact, getting pregnant with Joyce was a last-ditch attempt by their mother to keep the relationship together.

At first, this seemed to work well. Their marriage was better than it had been in years. But as the children grew older, and problems began to creep back into the marriage, Joyce's father turned all his attention on Joyce as a form of escape. In almost no time, a bond was set up between Joyce and her father that grew to exclusive proportions.

Joyce's father smothered his daughter with affection and attention. His lonely wife and son saw this all too clearly. As the years went on, Joyce became her father's best friend, encourager, confidante, and companion, and all the time the rest of the family languished in neglect.

How did Jim respond? He responded like many other children who see a sibling gain all a parent's attention. Like Joseph's brothers, he became angry at his sister for stealing his father away and would do almost anything to gain back his attention. Unfortunately, that usually meant "acting up" or even breaking something in the house. At that point he would definitely get his father's attention, but he received an angry tirade rather than the tender response he sought. Rather than Jim's actions drawing his father close to him, they drove his dad even closer to his sister.

Jim faced another problem as well, a problem he shares with many people we see who have missed out on the blessing. He felt a nagging sense of insecurity about whether he was truly valuable as a person and worthy to be loved. His father could not be wrong, Jim reasoned, so the problem must lie within himself. This feeling deeply affected Jim and continued to color his thinking for years to come.

Tragically, the lack of his father's blessing led Jim to take one more hurtful step. Jim began to equate his lack of blessing with being a boy. Heaped on top of his pain at being rejected by his father was a growing sense of sexual confusion. He was so angry with his sister for gaining the blessing and at his mother for doing nothing about it, that all women became objects of dislike.

While he was not aware of it at the time, his deep longing for the missing blessing of his father left him like a wounded deer, easy prey to the advances of an older, homosexual man. For seven years, Jim tried to fill his lack of the blessing in homosexual relationships, reaping pain and emotional destruction as a result, not the freedom of choice that he thought he'd receive.

What about Joyce? Certainly she wouldn't have experienced these kinds of problems. After all, she had received what looked like the blessing from her father.

While all the elements of the blessing were showered on Joyce, her blessing was actually counterfeit, not real. Her father gave her the blessing only to meet *his* needs, not hers. As a result, she became so dependent on her father to meet her every need that she became emotionally enslaved to him.

When Joyce grew up and it was time to think of leaving home and of getting married, she couldn't fathom the thought. Her father had smothered her with so much attention that boys her own age paled in comparison. Her father even acted like a jealous rival, pointing out every flaw he could see in the young men Joyce dated. Instead of preparing her to "leave" home in a healthy way to "cleave" to another man, he smothered her so badly that he kept her from transferring her attachment to one. Even in her late twenties, she was kept an emotional adolescent, "not quite ready" to enter into an adult relationship with any other man.

Joyce had never learned to share or compromise, so all the relationships with men she did have were "disappointing" and short-lived. Joyce finally married in her early thirties; but only after her father picked out the man.

When we first saw Joyce in counseling, she had come in to complain about her husband. The "things he expected of her" were beyond her comprehension or willingness to give—things like supplying a little attention to meet *his* needs or her agreeing to meet her father for lunch only two times a week.

The problems that Jim and Joyce faced as adults began when they were young. Jim suffered from a lack of the blessing while Joyce struggled to cope with being flooded by it. Coming to grips with these facts was what first began to free them from this first home that can withhold the blessing, a home where the blessing falls on only one side of the mountain.

The Second Home: Where the Blessing Is Placed Just Out of Reach

Craig looked strangely out of place in the psychiatric ward where I (John) was a seminary intern. He was tall, athletic looking, and quite handsome. With his preppie clothes, he looked as if he belonged back on his university campus, not in the hospital; that is, until you looked at his wrists and saw the thick bandages wrapped around them.

Craig had been admitted to the hospital for attempting suicide. If his roommate had not unexpectedly come back to the dorm and found him, Craig would have succeeded. What was it that caused this young man so much pain that he felt he could no longer face the future? He grew up in a home where the blessing was always placed just out of reach.

Craig's father was a petroleum engineer who was considered a genius in his field. He demanded excellence from himself and expected nothing less from his family. As a result of his critical attitude and incredibly high expectations from his son, his blessing became like the mechanical rabbit at a dog race—running slow enough to excite the chase, but fast enough not to be caught.

Nothing Craig accomplished ever quite measured up to his father's standards. That was particularly true when it came to Craig's academic abilities. Craig had done well in school. He even received a partial scholarship to a good engineering school in the state. His father's only remark on this achievement was that it "wasn't a full scholarship" and that there were "better schools out of state he didn't hear from." What finally caused Craig to attempt to take his life was that for the first time in his three years at college, he was going to receive a *B* in a class.

Craig wanted his father's blessing so badly that he had studied diligently to be an *A* student, just like his father. And receiving his first *B* meant more to him than losing a perfect grade point. That *B* meant losing any chance at his father's blessing. This "failure" discouraged Craig so badly that the future was not worth facing.

When the blessing is held just out of reach, it can create tremendous problems for a child. While most people will not come to the point of trying to take their lives as

Craig did, almost every child who grows up in this type of home will be lured into a futile chase for his or her parents' blessing.

Robin was an example of someone who spent her life in pursuit of her parents' love and acceptance.

Robin's parents were both demanding. Her father was a successful businessman, and her mother was a leader in social circles. "Success" was a motto in their home and had something to do with every magazine they subscribed to. They demanded excellence from Robin and would only award praise or hugs upon a spectacular achievement. What these parents didn't realize by placing the blessing way up on the top shelf was that their daughter grew up in a terrible "double bind."

To try to please her father, Robin had majored in marketing in college, just as he had. She did quite well in school and landed a job with prestige and the chance for further advancement. Robin spent many extra hours at her job, and her father was quite pleased with her achievements.

Then Robin fell in love and married a junior partner in the company. After a few years, children were born to the couple. Immediately their two boys became the apple of their grandmother's eye. Robin's mother expected her daughter to do all the things with the children that she had done (forgetting that she had never worked during her marriage) and told Robin this constantly.

Soon Robin was being mercilessly pulled in two directions. To try to capture her father's blessing, she tried to keep the same pace at work that had won his praise in the past. But she didn't have two preschool children then. To try to reach her mother's blessing, Robin tried to be "supermom" and do everything with her children that a nonworking mother could do. After several years of a killing schedule, one day the pressure became too much. Like pressing too hard against a glass window, her emotional life shattered around her.

In the United States we live in a culture that is so "fast paced" that it makes it easy to be "driven" to the breaking point. Unfortunately, people who have missed out on the blessing are often susceptible to this kind of frenzied activity. In reaching for parental acceptance, they can become workaholics.

Workaholics seeking the blessing are found in the Christian community, and not just among those sitting in the pews. Many church leaders today are driven to do more and more to serve others. However, what is really driving them may be an attempt to gain acceptance from other people that they never received at home from their parents.

Forgetting about God's sovereignty and biblical passages concerning our need for a "Sabbath rest,"[1] many modern-day pastors will work themselves until they drop. In the process of helping so many people, they often receive "buckets" of praise and appreciation that are poured on their lives. However, instead of this praise fulfilling their missing blessing from the past, it actually creates the need to help even more people in order to somehow feel acceptable. This is exactly what happened to a friend of ours in the ministry who never received the blessing from his parents.

Pastor Rick was what many considered a model pastor. He had majored in Hebrew and theology in seminary and had still managed to win the preaching award for his class. He began his pastoral ministry working at a small church that had not grown at all in over fifteen years. Within two years he had tripled the attendance and had moved on to another church. Great success followed this move up the church growth ladder, and he was pushed even further into the Christian limelight. After four years at his second church, working day and night to minister to the congregation, he was offered the senior pastorate at a "mega-church" with a membership of several thousand people. For a pastor in his denomination, he was on top of the mountain of success looking down.

Everywhere Pastor Rick went, more and more people

would tell him how great he was. And he would feel more and more empty when they did. Television appearances and making the "conference circuit" could not fill his real needs, though. At the peak of his profession, at only forty-six years of age, he had a nervous breakdown and had to leave his church.

One major reason this happened was that crowds of people could never fill the lack of acceptance this man felt from his parents. His parents were not believers, and nothing he ever accomplished brought words of blessing from their lips. He had tried harder and harder to be the perfect minister, trying to prove to his parents that he was worth blessing; but their blessing never quite came within reach. His drive to fill that missing blessing with the praise of others left him emotionally broken and his life in ruins.

This man needed to deal honestly with the underlying forces that shaped him. Fortunately, he did. After four months of honestly looking at his life and of taking the time to re-introduce himself to the God who says, "My yoke is easy, and my burden is light," he was able to go back into the ministry with a whole new perspective. Because he was no longer driven to try to fill his need for personal acceptance through other people, for the first time in his years of ministry he was truly free to serve his congregation. He could finally enjoy God's acceptance for just breathing, not for trying to meet all the thousands of needs around him. His ministry, his wife, and his family blossomed as a result.

Through applying the same principles we will discover in a later chapter, this pastor discovered how to live a fulfilling life apart from his parents' blessing. He learned to drink from his heavenly Father's overflowing cup of blessing, rather than from his parents' empty cup. But he only did this by honestly coming to grips with his past, a past that included growing up in a home where the blessing was always just out of reach.

The Third Home: Where the Blessing Is Exchanged for a Burden

In some homes, a form of the blessing is given to a child, but at a terrible price. Read the words of one woman who wrote a letter to a national columnist. Her words speak of an incredible cost associated with gaining only a small part of the blessing:

> Ever since I was a little girl, my mother made me feel guilty if I did not do exactly as she wanted. Dozens of times she has said, "You will be sorry when I am in my coffin." I was never a bad girl. I always did everything she requested me to do. . . .
>
> Both my parents are eighty-two. One of these days my mother will die, and I am terrified of what it will do to me.[2]

This poor woman has paid a tremendous price for her blessing—her very life. A blessing she is not even sure she has received. One certainly can't say she didn't try hard enough. Did you catch her words? "I was never a bad girl. I always did everything she requested me to do." In spite of all her efforts, she received a burden instead of a blessing.

In this third home that withholds the blessing, a terrible transaction takes place. A child is coaxed by guilt or fear into giving up all rights to his or her goals and desires. In return, the child gets a blessing that lasts only until the parent's next selfish desire beckons to be met. So it was with Nicole, a woman who had to carry around a terrible secret in order to keep her blessing.

When Nicole was only nine years old, her parents divorced. After a whirlwind romance, her mother remarried in less than six months; and a stepfather moved into the house. While Nicole's mother was away at work one evening, her stepfather came into her room. What started out in his words to be "playing" became an evening of shame and horror for Nicole. Like thousands of young girls her age, she became the victim of sexual abuse.

The next morning, her stepfather pulled Nicole aside and told her that if she ever mentioned what had happened to anyone, he would divorce her mother, beat her within an inch of her life, and leave her and her mother to "starve on the street." On the other hand, if she told no one, he would accept her and be nice to her and her mother.

The fear of what would happen to her mother, added to her own feelings of shame, kept her quiet. Because Nicole never mentioned to her mother what happened, her stepfather kept his part of the bargain. He went on with his life and marriage as though nothing had ever happened. He even treated her decently after that one event.

In remaining quiet to keep her stepfather's favor, Nicole paid a terrible price. Over the years, she was emotionally held hostage in her own home. In error, she believed her silence would buy her stepfather's blessing for her and her mother. Only later did she realize a man like her stepfather gives only a curse.

When we first met Nicole, she was married and the mother of three children. For years she had been living in another state and only infrequently saw her mother and stepfather. To keep her parents together, she had paid a terrible price. Unable to share her deepest hurt and pain out loud, her painful memories shouted to her day and night to right this wrong. Only when she broke down and shared her secret with her loving husband did she begin to find freedom from this past burden.

Parents who hold out the elements of the blessing to their child with such strings attached do them a grave disservice. They are using one of the most powerful needs in the human heart to lure a child to the web of their own selfish needs.

Nicole and others like her can receive a genuine blessing. Nicole first saw this in the patient, loving attitude of her husband. Then she believed it when she discovered for the first time her heavenly Father's love, with no strings attached.

If we are carrying a great burden to gain our parents' blessing, or if we are expecting it of our children, we need to understand that we are giving or receiving a counterfeit blessing. The blessing we saw in the Old Testament was not purchased at such a terrible cost. The blessing was a gift that was given, not something that was earned. Like God's love, it is an act of unmerited favor and unconditional acceptance and is bestowed upon a person of high value.

In spite of the problems that were a part of their homes, Joyce, Jim, Craig, Robin, Pastor Rick, and even Nicole were able to work through missing out on the blessing. They discovered, as we all will in a later chapter, that help and hope are available for anyone who grew up in a similar situation. However, we still need to visit two more homes that commonly withhold the blessing. Then we will look at the help these people discovered. In our first stop, we will see a home displaying a banner marked "Unyielding Traditions Live Here."

—9—

Homes That Withhold the Blessing: Part 2

☙❧

---

*J*im was confused and brokenhearted. At nineteen he had been ordered out of his parents' home by his father, and he didn't know where to turn. What was the problem? Was it open rebellion? Lying? Stealing?

Actually, for Jim's father, it was something even worse. Jim had a role he was expected to fulfill in his family, and Jim had decided it was a mold he did not fit. Such an attitude is an unpardonable sin in homes that fly the banner, "Unyielding Traditions Live Here." In this home the blessing is only given when these traditions are met.

Jim's father was a minister. His grandfather was a minister. Even his great-grandfather was a minister! Three generations of Smiths had heard the call to the ministry early in life and unquestioningly responded to it. Now it was the fourth generation's turn. Jim's older brother had decided to go into the ministry and was attending the seminary his father had attended. However, with Jim the pattern was about to be broken.

Jim had trusted Christ as his Lord and Savior early in life, and he had grown in his love for the Lord over the years. He was attending a Christian college in his hometown and dating another minister's daughter. Up to this point, Jim had fulfilled the prescribed plan for a Smith. Seminary would certainly be right around the corner, and then a small pastorate to continue his family's tradition.

Then Jim told his parents of a decision that left them angry and upset. When Jim had to declare his major in college, he had chosen marketing over missions.

Jim's father was mortified. Having three generations of Smiths in the ministry and both his sons in seminary or pre-seminary training had been such a good illustration in sermons and at conferences. Now he was in jeopardy of losing his bragging rights. All because a rebellious son dared to question the unquestionable, something that Smiths could not do.

At first, his girlfriend was suspected of luring Jim away from his calling; but that proved to be false. His closest friends were all believers, and little evidence could be amassed that a conspiracy had been launched from that direction. No, it came down to Jim himself. In an angry session in the living room after dinner one night, he and his father exchanged angry words. When Jim would not admit that it was sin in his life that had led him astray, his father "invoked discipline" on his erring son. Jim was ordered to separate himself from his family until he had repented of the error of his ways.

Sound incredible? This separation happens every day to a son or daughter who breaks an unbreakable family tradition. We have seen it with a son who refused to take over his father's garage and with a daughter who didn't marry into the right social class. This type separation has surfaced with someone else's son who dared to vote Republican and with another daughter who turned down a bid to join her mother's sorority.

In each of the examples above, the parents felt cheated out of something they expected from their children. As a result, they have withheld or taken back their blessing from that child as punishment.

This fourth home that withholds the blessing, like the other homes we have looked at, causes problems for each child in the family. This home can force a brother to "choose sides" with his parents against another brother and force one sister to sneak out at night to visit another. For erring sons or daughters, it can ruin every holiday and special family event because of the layer of ice that forms the moment they walk in the door.

We need to be clear about what kind of parents we are looking at who foster such actions. We are not talking about the kind of parents who grieve over a son or daughter who has strayed into legitimate error and who are, for that reason, forced to keep the child at arm's length—parents like Eddie and Belle.

Eddie and Belle's oldest son, Don, was an alcoholic. He had started drinking in Vietnam by turning to the bottle to try to deaden the horrors of war. When he returned home, he had continued to drink as an escape from facing the struggles of re-entry into civilian life.

Don met and married a young lady in less than four months, and within a year she had given birth to their first child. Unable to keep a decent job over the years and drinking more than ever, Don began to take out his frustrations on his wife and children. At one point things became so bad that his wife had to get a restraining order against him to protect herself and the children.

Don's destructive behavior broke his parents' hearts. They prayed for him daily and tried to be both counselors and encouragers. They had bailed him out financially innumerable times, and they had even bailed him out of jail on two occasions.

Throughout his struggles, Don's parents had never withheld their blessing. They never approved of his behavior, and they had told him so; but he was their son, and they loved him deeply. Yet when he began physically abusing his family, they made the painful decision to withhold financial support from Don, unless he attended an alcoholic treatment program.

Eddie and Belle shared their decision with their son in love, and he exploded in anger. Calling them every name under the sun, he said they had betrayed him. He threatened to get even and stormed out of the house.

Don's parents did not stop loving their son. Yet because they loved him and wanted the best for him as a person even more than they loved their relationship with him, they were willing to confront him and risk losing him for a season. They withheld one aspect of the blessing from their son because of the destructive problems he faced. Both biblically and relationally they were on firm ground to withhold that portion of their blessing from their son.

Such parents do not qualify to have the banner "Unyielding Family Traditions" raised over their home. Their tough love displays too much maturity, personal integrity, and courage. The kind of house that deserves this banner is reserved for people like Jerry and Helen who withheld every bit of their blessing from their daughter for reasons as solid as quicksand.

Brenda was a charming, intelligent young lady who deeply loved her parents. They cared for her too and had the material resources to express that affection in tangible ways—new clothes, new cars, the finest schools. These were hers until she met and fell in love with Brent.

Brent was attending the same distinguished school that Brenda was. But Brent was paying his own way. He was doing extremely well and had a bright future ahead of him.

Brent and Brenda met the first day of school at the sorority house where Brent was "hashing" (cooking and cleaning up) to pay for his meals. Both Brenda and Brent were new believers in Christ, and they found out they had many interests in common. Their relationship began as a close friendship, but by the end of school it had developed into a deep love for each other.

They were each sure that a summer off from dating would end their infatuation with each other; but after dozens of letters back and forth and phone bills so high that they could have provided the money to add two new stories to the Southwestern Bell office, they knew they had been smitten with the real thing. By December of the next year they were talking engagement, and it was time for Brent to meet Brenda's parents.

Brent's mother lived near the college, and Brenda had seen her numerous times. Already, a deep affection was growing between these two. Brent's father had died in an automobile accident when Brent was just a boy, and his mother had raised him by working in a local grade school cafeteria. Brenda felt at home with Brent's mother, and she just knew her parents would welcome Brent with open arms. Nothing could have been further from the truth.

Brenda was so in love with Brent that she had failed to see the hardening attitude of her parents regarding their relationship. Not wanting to push her further into the relationship by forbidding it, they had hoped by hosting parties and taking her to the club where all the "nice boys" were she would break off the relationship on her own. The little they had heard about Brent's background had been more than enough. He would never, under any circumstances, enter their home much less become their son-in-law. Her parents had too much at stake when it came to their daughter's social standing, and their own.

Brenda was shattered when she received this message. Brent was sitting right in the room with her when she called her parents. She and Brent had been so excited to "break the news" that he was coming home with her to ask for her hand in marriage. However, in only a few minutes this couple's hopes had turned to ashes. Brenda could *not* bring him home, and she was to stop seeing him or lose her parents' financial backing at school.

Brent and Brenda tried to pick up the pieces of their shattered dreams. Brenda made a trip home to see if she could change her parents' attitude. She could not. They only repeated the firm warning that too much was at stake for her to throw it all away on someone who "didn't deserve" her or her family.

Brent and Brenda sought counsel from their pastor and close friends, and even called on Brenda's family's pastor to ask his advice. Yet heaven and earth were not sufficient to move her parents' ultimatum one inch.

Brenda explained to her parents that she felt the Lord

had brought Brent and her together. Like everyone at the club, Brenda's parents went to church; but the God they knew would never approve of such a social outcast. If being poor were not enough, he was even a Yankee to top it off. In their minds, God's blessing, as well as their own, would never rest on such a person.

To try to honor Brenda's parents, Brent and Brenda put off their engagement and marriage for a year and a half. Still, any attempt for Brent to meet her parents face to face or to discuss the issue was stopped before it began.

With a semester of school left, Brenda made the most difficult decision in her life, a decision she is still paying for almost seven years later. She and Brent were married at a lovely service in a small university chapel, with only Brent's mother representing their parents. Brenda took a part-time job at the school bookstore to help pay for her final semester and graduation.

Brenda's parents have been out to see Brenda and Brent two times over the past seven years. Each time they have come to see a new grandchild for a few days. Yet their bitter rejection has never let up. By withholding their blessing on Brenda's marriage—even years after the wedding itself—they have won a hollow victory. They lost the battle when it came to whom their daughter married, but they win the war every lonely day and unhappy holiday that Brenda faces without their love and support.

It could be debated that Brent and Brenda should have never married in the first place, especially without her parents' blessing. However, to remain bitter, resentful and unwilling to make contact with their daughter or her husband—even seven years after their wedding—shows a desire to punish, not to stand on principle.

Without question, one of the greatest gifts parents can give their child is their blessing when it comes to that child's marriage. When parents withhold the blessing from their children for cheating them out of a "high church" wedding, or for marrying a Greek instead of a

Czech, a German instead of an Italian, or for choosing to attend First Presbyterian rather than Second Baptist, they hit below the belt.

We are not talking about parents who agonize over their believing son who is set on marrying an unbelieving woman or the parents who face the possibility that their never-married daughter may marry a man fresh from his fifth divorce. Yet even in these situations parents can still demonstrate love for their child in spite of disapproving of his or her actions.

Homes that wave the banner "Unyielding Traditions Live Here" do not consider right and wrong—only tradition. They know full well the impact of their punitive decision to withhold their blessing—and that is exactly why they do it. Their pride has been hurt, now their children will hurt as well. As the years go by, the parents' position can harden. They are unwilling to give an inch, as if doing so meant giving a mile. They can sit through sermon after sermon about forgiveness in church, never once misunderstanding what the pastor says, but still refuse to put their son's or daughter's picture back on the mantle.

In these homes, fulfill every expectation, and the blessing will be given. Travel a different road, and expect to wander far from the shelter of acceptance. This is the fourth home that commonly withholds the blessing, and it can leave a child emotionally in a place where it is always winter, never spring.

The Fifth Home: Receiving Only a Part of the Blessing

In this final home, a child does receive the blessing, but only in part. There are several ways in which this can happen, and each has the power to leave a child feeling only half-blessed. We will look at three common situations where a part of the blessing can be withheld: divorce, desertion, and adoption.

WHEN PARENTS DIVORCE

In previous chapters, we have discussed the effects that an "emotional divorce" can have on a child. This situation happens when one parent withholds the blessing from a child or spouse, yet the marriage stays together. It is equally difficult for children to handle when the parents actually do divorce, regardless of the age of the children when the divorce takes place.

In the typical scenario that surrounds a divorce, the wife will retain custody of the children and the father will move out. Studies have shown that during the first year following a divorce, many fathers see their children on a regular schedule. In fact, the "Sugardaddy" syndrome appears quite frequently.

This syndrome occurs when the father smothers the children with gifts and attention right after the divorce. As a result, the children may feel closer to him than they have in years. (The one who usually has difficulty during this time is the mother who is struggling to make ends meet and has to compete with lavish gifts and trips for the children, which she cannot afford.)

Unfortunately, such attention is usually temporary, and typically after one year the contact between father and child will begin to decrease. By the time three years have gone by, many fathers will see their son or daughter once a month or less.

Many of these children grow up experiencing only part of the blessing. They have the consistency of their mother's blessing and also the constant longing for the missing blessing of their father. When the flood of initial attention from their father slows down to only a trickle, anger, insecurity, and misbehavior can often result.

The blessing a father gives his child is just as important as the blessing the child's mother extends. When it is absent, there is going to be a vacuum present in that child's life, a vacuum that needs to be filled.

We want to stress one important point to the parent remaining at home who consistently gives his or her child the blessing. (This point is also important to consider for parents of children who were deserted or adopted.) Children will naturally long for the blessing of the absent parent, regardless of the situation surrounding the divorce. Their desire for that missing element does not negate or point out any flaws in the way they are loved by their custodial parent. Almost all children have an emotional need to re-establish connection with the other person responsible for their birth.

I (John) found this to be true in my life. My mother and father divorced when I was a little over thirteen months old. My mother retained custody of my older brother, my twin brother, and me, which gave her three children under three years of age to raise.

As I have had the opportunity later in life to look through "How to" books on single parenting, I discovered that my mother could have been on the cover. To this day, I cannot remember her running down my father verbally or erecting walls that would keep us from contacting him. This was true even in the first years after the divorce when she had to go to work.

My mother worked full time as an executive at a major savings and loan, yet her nights and weekends reflected her commitment to us children. On dozens of Friday nights, she would stuff us all in her car, hook on our little "teardrop" trailer, and off we would go to the mountains in northern Arizona or to the beach in Mexico to camp out with other families.

Camping was an acquired interest for my mother. Coming from an affluent home in Indiana, her only camping had been at Holiday Inns next to a campsite. Yet she knew that three growing boys needed the rigors of outdoor life and the male companionship of several married friends who treated each child in the "camping club" as their own.

I can say without question that my brothers and I learned about the blessing long before we could read about it in the Scriptures. From meaningful touching, to attaching high value to us, to picturing a special future for each son—we learned the elements of the blessing by experiencing them. My mother is a very loving person; but she is also very wise. Wise enough not to question how adequate her love was, when after several years, my father sought to re-establish contact with us.

Today, my brothers and I enjoy a growing relationship with our father and still are very close to our mother. We have these good relations in large part because the natural desire to make contact with our father was not held against us. The blessing of both of my parents has never been used as a bargaining chip to play one against the other. Even in a home situation that is less than God's ideal, we have found help to make up for missing a part of the blessing.

We realize that not all divorces and parental relationships end up like the story described above. In part, that is why we will spend an entire chapter talking about how we deal with the lack of a blessing. However, we would like to share two other avenues for helping single-parent families in particular.

Two programs at our church have proved particularly helpful for single-parent families. The first is a "Big Brother/Little Brother, Big Sister/Little Sister" program designed to provide for the needs of boys and girls who are missing the elements of the blessing from a mother or father. By matching an adult male with a young boy and an adult female with a young girl, gaping holes caused by a missing parental blessing can begin to be filled.

The second program is an "Adopt a Grandparent" program that matches a single-parent child (or even children whose grandparents live out of state), with a member of the seniors' department. Often, these godly, older saints can provide a little boy or girl a precious commodity. As one little six-year-old commented, "Grandparents are the only adults who have time to listen." Match these children with a senior who needs to be needed, and each can become a source of blessing to the other.

Any parents who are considering divorce need to face

facts squarely. Splitting apart a marriage can severely affect each child in a negative way. While these children can learn to live without the blessing of both parents, a growing marriage is the best place for it to be given and developed.

WHEN ONE PARENT DESERTS THE FAMILY

Desertion by a parent can be harder on a child than losing him or her to death. When a parent dies, a child knows that in this life the opportunity to regain a missing part of the blessing from that parent is gone. When a parent deserts his or her children, they know that "out there somewhere" is a living person who still has the power to bless. Some children can catch a glimpse of that missing person's face in an airport or on a crowded street. But when they run to get a closer look, the likeness disappears, and they are left face to face with a stranger.

When a father or mother suddenly, unexpectedly, deserts the family, it can have serious effects on a child. In a seminar we attended on the effects on "displaced" children, one of the speakers used this quotation:

> The father who deserts his family suddenly and never sees them again can leave a daughter forever afraid to allow herself to be vulnerable to a man, sure that he too will leave her. . . . His daughter's resulting anger may give her trouble with men all her life. She may totally avoid men, or keep seeking the father she never had.[1]

With the Lord's help, such a prediction does not have to become a reality. However, nagging questions can remain in the mind of a child whose parents just walk out, questions Laurie asked herself for years.

Laurie's mother had walked out on her family. Surprisingly, wives' leaving their families is not an uncommon occurrence any more. One popular secular book that noted this fact was even titled *The Runaway Wives*.

Laurie's mother was having an affair with her supervisor at work. When he was transferred across the country, she packed her bags one day when the rest of the family was gone and went with him. She did not leave a note written to Laurie, or even call to talk to her. Her mother just sent a certified letter that arrived addressed to Laurie's father, delivering notice of a pending divorce.

Laurie and her father did very well together through the grade school and high school years. She even went to secretarial school and landed a nice job as an executive assistant. Yet lurking in the shadows every time Laurie became serious in a dating relationship was a nagging fear deep inside.

Every time Laurie would think seriously about marriage or having a family, a little voice would say, "Don't do it. You'll be just like your mother and leave them too." The counsel of a helpful pastor and learning about how God could meet the missing part of her blessing finally helped her be able to marry and set up a happy family.

Desertion leaves so many important questions unanswered. It is a cruel dealer who passes out only half the cards a child needs to gain the blessing.

DEALING WITH THE QUESTIONS
RAISED BY ADOPTION

We see yet another group of children in counseling who commonly struggle with gaining only part of the blessing. These are adopted children who struggle with the question, "Why did my natural parents leave me?"

We know many parents of adopted children who do a tremendous job of giving them the blessing. These parents more than make up for any loss a child might feel by being separated from his or her natural parents, especially if the child was adopted quite young. However, in even the best of homes where a child is totally secure in his adoptive parents' love, the question can still arise: "Why did my natural parents leave me?"

Sometimes this questioning comes in the form of misbehaving to see if his or her adoptive parents will "leave me like my natural parents did." These children will test the limits of their adoptive parents' commitment in an attempt to reassure themselves that they really are loved.

Other children will join clubs or pay organizations to find their natural parents, all in an attempt to regain that part of the blessing they lost in years past or to hear it one last time.

Adoptive parents should expect some behavior of this sort, especially when the child gets old enough to ask such questions for himself or herself. However, by providing the five elements of the blessing, backed by God's unchanging love, adopted children can have the security and self-confidence to face these questions in a healthy way. They may still ask the questions, but they are not dependent on their natural parents' blessing to lay the foundation for their lives. God's love, demonstrated through providing them the blessing, can bring them the certainty they need about themselves and the certainty that they belong to a family that truly loves them.

We have looked at five different homes that we commonly see in counseling that withhold the blessing from their children. As each home is different in how it does this, each child's response to missing the blessing can be unique as well.

Withholding the blessing can be a powerful shaping tool for a child's life, just as bestowing it can be powerful. As we close this chapter and pull together what we have learned, let's look at seven types of children who come out of homes without the blessing.

Without the Blessing, Children Can Become . . .

THE SEEKERS

We have looked at several examples where children have reacted to missing the blessing by beginning a life-long search. Seekers are people who are always searching for intimacy, but are seldom able to tolerate it. These are the people who feel tremendous fulfillment in the thrill of a courtship. But after marriage, their lack of acceptance from their parents leaves them uncomfortable in receiving it from a spouse. Never sure of how acceptance "feels," they are never satisfied with wearing it too long in a relationship. They can even struggle with believing in God's unchanging love for them because of the lack of permanence in the blessing in their early lives.

THE SHATTERED

These are the people whose lives are deeply troubled over the loss of their parents' love and acceptance. Fear, anxiety, depression, and emotional withdrawal many times can be traced to a person's missing out on his or her family's blessing. Their unhappy road can even lead them to the terrifying cliffs of suicide, convinced they are destined to be a "Cipher in the Snow."

THE SMOTHERERS

Like a two-thousand-pound sponge, these people react to missing their parents' blessing by sucking every bit of life and energy from a spouse, child, friend, or entire congregation. They are left so emotionally empty from their past that they smother other persons with their unmet needs and, like a parasite, drain these others of their desire to listen or help.

Unfortunately, when the other persons trying to make up for years of unmet needs finally tire of carrying these smothering persons' entire emotional weight, the message the smothering persons receive is that they are being rejected. Deeply hurt once again, they never realize that they have brought this pain upon themselves. They end up pushing away the blessing other people offer when actually they desperately need it.

THE ANGRY

As long as people are angry at each other, they are chained to each other. Many adults are still emotionally chained to their parents because they are angry over missing the blessing. They have never forgiven or forgotten. As a result, the rattle and chafing of emotional chains distract them from intimacy in other relationships. Many children thus go into life with a chip on their shoulders put there early in life when they believed they could never experience love and acceptance in their homes.

THE DETACHED

An old proverb says, "Once burned, twice shy." This motto is used by some children who have missed out on the blessing. After losing the blessing from an important person in their lives *once,* they spend a lifetime protecting themselves from its ever happening again. Keeping a spouse, children, or a close friend at arm's length, they protect themselves all right—at the price of inviting loneliness to take up residence in their lives.

THE DRIVEN

In this category line up extreme perfectionists, workaholics, notoriously picky housecleaners, and generally demanding people who go after getting their blessing the old-fashioned way: they try to "Earrrrrrrrn it." The only problem is that the blessing is a *gift;* you cannot buy the blessing. You can find some counterfeit blessings that are for sale—at an incredible price—but they last only as long as the "showroom shine" on a new car. In real life travels, such counterfeit blessings rust and corrode once they leave the showroom floor. Missing their parents' blessing challenges these driven people to attack a windmill named "accomplishment" in an illusory attempt to gain love and acceptance.

THE SEDUCED

Many people who have missed out on their parents' blessing look for that lost love in all the wrong places. As we mentioned in an earlier chapter, unmet needs for love and acceptance can tempt a person toward sexual immorality—all in an attempt to try to meet legitimate needs in an illegitimate way. Also in this category fall substance abusers. All too often, a drink or a pill is taken initially to try to cover up the hurt from empty relationships in the past or present. Alcoholism or drug abuse can become a counterfeit way to try to gain the deep emotional warmth that is a part of experiencing the elements of the blessing.[2]

In a recent study of compulsive gamblers (especially those struck with "lottery fever"), over 90 percent of the men studied were found to have "dismal childhoods, characterized by loneliness and rejection."[3] In other words, missing out on the elements of the blessing in a home can seduce a child into choosing immoral relationships, alcoholism, or even compulsive gambling as an attempt to fill missing relationship needs.

There is help to leave the ranks of those above and join the ranks of "the blessed." That help begins by discovering the reality of a spiritual family blessing that our Lord holds out to everyone and being willing to courageously face the past.

As we look past these homes that withhold the blessing, we will discover that every one of the elements of the blessing we might have missed out on can be ours. Rather than being locked into repeating the past, we can be free to grow into the people God wants us to be.

We shouldn't look down and lose hope if we grew up without the blessing. We should look up instead to the incredible provision of a blessing for our lives that can leave our lives overflowing, the kind of blessing that can even replace a curse with contentment.

—10—

Learning to Live Apart from the Blessing

~~~

Several years ago, I (John) counseled with the parents of a very disturbed twenty-one-year-old named Dean. Even though the problems these parents faced had existed for some time, they had put off coming in for help.

Dean had serious mental problems that had placed a tremendous burden on his family. Often he was angry and belligerent, occasionally becoming violent. Yet life had not always been so damaging for this family.

Dean's problems first began to develop after a car accident when he was eleven years old. The accident occurred soon after the family moved to Texas. Before the accident, when they were living in Michigan, Dean and his family had gotten along beautifully. In fact, they were a model family at the church they attended and in their community.

When Dean's behavior began to change following the accident, his concerned parents took him to specialist after specialist. They always received the same diagnosis: their son's problem had no medical solution. Perhaps time and understanding would work things out.

Dean's mother loved him dearly. Even when he was mad and sullen, she would spend hours trying to reason with him and read him verses of Scripture to make an impression on his life. Always she hoped that his "thorn in the flesh" would be removed and that their lives would be restored to what they were before the accident.

With Dean's brothers and sisters, and even with her husband, Dean's mother would constantly downplay the severity of her son's problems. In an attempt to alleviate the mounting pressure because of Dean's behavior, she would often set up family socials and special holiday events. She wanted to re-create a time when the whole family could be "all together again, just like in Michigan." However, as soon as Dean arrived on the scene, he would ruin the party with his angry words.

This loving mother refused to acknowledge that Dean's problems were as bad as they were. Her husband and the rest of the family could think what they wanted to; she knew that things would get better. Life would once again be just like it was "in Michigan." She even dreamed about this—until one day her dreams turned into a nightmare.

Dean's father was nearing retirement age, and he and his wife were looking forward to his retirement. This couple had been good stewards of the money God had entrusted to them, and they had saved a sizable nest egg to buy that dream retirement property up in the mountains.

Six months before Dad officially retired, Dean's parents called their realtor and said it was time to put their house on the market. They had talked this over with their children, and each of them was excited for their parents—all except Dean. Even though he had been living on his own for several years, he still made his parents' home his headquarters. This was almost a necessity because his violent temper had driven off every roommate and all but the staunchest friends.

When Dean came to his parents' home one night and saw the "For Sale" sign in their yard, he went berserk. He banged on the door repeatedly, but his parents were not at home. Finally, he pulled up the sign from the front yard and used it to bash in the glass in the front door window. Then he proceeded to tear up the house.

Dean's parents returned home several hours later. Chairs were overturned and lamps had been smashed. Dean had even ripped an inside tree out of the planter box and had stuck the "For Sale" sign in its place. Upstairs and down, the house was in a shambles. Yet of all the things that Dean had done, one thing literally broke his mother's heart. In fact, nothing he could have done to her home could have shattered her as much.

In his anger over their plan to move to a retirement home, Dean had gone into the hall where all the family pictures hung and cut every one of them into pieces. From baby pictures on up to their last family portrait with all the grandchildren, each one was torn beyond repair.

Dean's mother, like every parent, had treasured her children's pictures. They were irreplaceable and beyond price to her, especially the pictures of the family before Dean's accident. They had always given her hope that one day things would be just like before, just like "in Michigan."

Dean's mother learned a very painful lesson that night. A lesson that many people have to come to grips with who have missed out on the blessing from their parents, their spouse, a loved one, or a friend.

Dean's mother finally had to recognize and acknowledge that she now lived in Texas and life would never be like it was "in Michigan." Even if Dean made a dramatic recovery, things were not and could not be exactly the way they were. Instead of living with the dreams that Dean's problems would go away, or trying to convince herself that the last ten years of Dean's outbursts "really weren't that bad," she was forced to come to grips with the past and take responsibility for dealing with her problem in the present.

We see this same twofold tendency in person after person who has missed out on his or her parents' blessing. Many will try to explain away and put off admitting the obvious in their lives. Drawing imaginary pictures of their past or denying the real problems that exist can often keep them from honestly facing their past and their parents. By protecting themselves or their parents, they effectively prevent a cure.

If we never face the fact that we missed out on the blessing, we can postpone dealing with the pain of the past, but we can never avoid it. The legitimate pain of honestly dealing with this situation is what leads to healing and life. When we try to avoid this legitimate pain, we are actually laying on top of it layers of illegitimate pain.

Dean's mother refused to make the painful acknowledgement that her son had a serious problem, and she ended up suffering an even worse pain of guilt, anguish, and remorse. People who put off coming to grips with their past often reap the same kind of harvest, a harvest where pain is multiplied and sorrows doubled, all because they did not face the legitimate pain that comes with facing the truth.

In the pages that follow, we want to recommend several things that can help people who are suffering from missing out on the blessing (or help those who work with them). These recommendations are not a simple formula, nor do they guarantee an instant cure. However, in counseling men and women all across the country, we find that many who have applied these principles have received hope and healing.

The road to blessing that we would like to point people toward begins with the very difficult first step we tried to illustrate with Dean's mother. We need to be honest with ourselves.

Begin by Being Honest with Yourself

John 8:32 is a verse in the Scriptures that we require our counselees to memorize. Jesus is talking in this verse, and He says, "And you shall know the truth, and the truth shall make you free." The truth Jesus is talking about in this verse refers to knowing Him in all His purity. Christ offers no cover-ups, no denying there is a problem when there really is one. When we know the truth, we are walking in the light that exposes darkness; and it alone can begin to set us free.

Many of us need to turn on truth's searchlight and shine it on our past. Only then can we be free to walk confidently into the future. Greg was able to do this, and it paid rich dividends in his life.

Greg was four years old when his parents told him that a new little brother or sister was on the way. As with most four-year-olds, nine months seemed like nine years as he waited for his new playmate.

The day finally came when Greg's mother left for the hospital, and he knew he wouldn't have to wait much longer. That next day, Greg went with his father to the hospital to see his new baby sister. However, when Greg came into his mother's hospital room, he had a surprise. He had two baby sisters, two beautiful twin girls who were already becoming the apples of their mother's eye.

Greg was certainly not loved any less when the twins came home, but things had definitely changed. Big brother was now having to share his parents' time and attention with not only one sister, but two. When the twins got older, things became even worse from Greg's perspective. The same people who stopped his mother to comment on how cute the little girls were in their double stroller rarely lifted their eyes to notice an older brother longing for the same affirmation.

Greg's parents loved him deeply. In no way did they intentionally try to overlook Greg or cater to the twins. Also, Greg loved his sisters. He was the perfect big brother, looking out for his charges and showing them the ropes when they got into school. Yet as the years went by, even the special bond between the twin girls became a minor source of jealousy for Greg. He just could not compete with the special closeness between his two look-alike sisters, and it bothered him.

Long after he and his sisters were grown and out of the house, Greg attended one of our seminars where he heard for the first time about the family blessing. In many ways, Greg knew that he was loved and accepted and that his parents had tried hard to provide him the blessing. Yet in his heart of hearts, he questioned whether he had really received it after the twins were born. For years he had had a nagging insecurity in his life that he could trace directly back to this fact.

Greg knew that all his family would soon be gathering at his parents' house to celebrate the holidays. After the conference ended, he also knew that he needed to deal honestly with his feelings of missing out on at least a part of the blessing. With every bit of courage he had, Greg decided he would bring up the subject with his parents.

The first morning he was at their home, the opportunity came up for him to discuss his feelings with his parents. The three of them were alone at the breakfast table; everyone else had gone out shopping for Christmas ornaments or a last-minute present.

Greg began talking with his parents by sharing with them much of what he had learned about the blessing at the seminar. The concept was new to them as well, and they perked up and got right into the discussion.

He then took several minutes to praise his parents and thank them for the way they had put into practice several elements of the blessing.

Finally, he brought up his feelings of missing out on part of the blessing when the twins had come along. In a loving, nonaccusatory fashion, he shared one of the deepest secrets of his heart with his parents.

As soon as Greg began sharing his concern, his mother began to cry. Greg immediately tried to comfort her and told her he wished he had never brought it up. "No!" said his mother. "Please don't be sorry. I've wanted to talk about this for so long. I've always thought it might have bothered you, but I didn't know how to bring it up."

Almost instantly, Greg and his parents were drawn into unity. They cried and laughed and hugged each other as if they had just been introduced after years of being apart, and in fact they had.

That night the now grown children and their parents

sat down for a family council. Something they hadn't done in years. The topic of conversation at the breakfast table that morning was shared with the twins, and they had their chance to cry, to share, and to reaffirm their love for their brother and their parents. Any nagging guilt they had over the situation was now resolved and turned into gratitude for a courageous older brother.

By Greg's willingness to share his feelings honestly with his parents and his twin sisters, if ever a part of the blessing had been missing in his life, it had certainly been filled up. Greg was even more confident at work in the weeks that followed, something that his employer noticed almost immediately.

We can't stress how important it is to be honest with your feelings regarding missing the blessing. It is the important first step toward healing and restoration.

Seek to Understand Your Parents' Background

The next recommendation we make to anyone who has missed out on his or her family's blessing is to understand as much as they can about their parents' background. Following this one bit of advice can free many people from wondering why they never received the blessing.

At the time we are writing this chapter, there is a comedian on many television commercials whom we love to watch. He plays an incredibly clumsy "hick" who is constantly pestering his pal, Verne. Whenever he wants Verne to remember something really important (like the particular product he is endorsing), he has a line that goes, "Tattoo that on your brain, Verne." Well, here is a principle that we hope people who have missed out on the blessing will "tattoo on their brains": In the vast majority of cases, parents who do not give the blessing never received it themselves.

Andrea took this advice to heart, and it totally changed her perspective on her father. Andrea heard about the concept of the blessing at a singles retreat we did. For years she had struggled with how distant her father seemed to her. He was always cordial to her, and he never raised his voice with any of the children. But what was missing left Andrea with nagging questions about whether she had received the blessing. Besides an occasional hug, her father had not demonstrated, to her way of thinking, any of the five elements of the blessing she had learned about.

Andrea was still living at home, and she took the first opportunity she could after the retreat to talk to her father about what she had learned. (What Andrea found out in that conversation was a key to understanding her father, the key she had never known before.)

After her father had listened to his daughter talk about the blessing (he was always a good listener, just not a good talker), he cleared his throat and shared with Andrea something of his past. For the first time her father told Andrea about his past in some detail. Perhaps she simply had not asked before or maybe he had never volunteered, but Andrea gained a better picture of her father's home that day than she ever had before.

Andrea had never met her grandparents on her father's side. They had both died a few years before she was born. And as he had been an only child, her father had no brothers or sisters to become aunts and uncles to pass down family stories.

Andrea's father had grown up in England and his parents were very British. Apparently, they even held claim to a small title of nobility.

When their son, Andrea's father, was born, he was raised with all the dignity and care afforded any English citizen of high birth. During his early years, he had a nanny who helped raise him, while his parents kept the respectable distance proper for teaching children discipline and manners. His relationship with his parents was so formal, anytime he addressed his father it was to be prefaced by "Sir." No using "Dad," "Daddy," "Papa," or anything of the kind in this household. "Sir" was the proper form of address.

In addition to the requirement to formally address his parents, meaningful touching was strictly taboo, and words of praise were as rare as hen's teeth (which, in case you weren't raised on a farm, are quite rare).

In the course of one hour, Andrea learned more about her father's background than she had in the nineteen previous years. As a result of seeing how her father was raised, she gained a new compassion and understanding for his actions toward her and her brothers and sisters. She even found out that compared to his parents, her father felt he was a fanatic in trying to make sure each of his children received the blessing. And all the time she thought he was withholding it!

If we will stop and take the time to look beyond our parents' actions in the present and back at their past, it will be time well spent. As we will see in a later chapter, often we will find out that our parents need the elements of the blessing from us just as much (or more) than we need these elements from them!

Understand That Even a Curse Can Be Changed into a Blessing

Some children have a difficult time relating to the concept of a family blessing. From their perspective, they have received a curse from a mother or father in place of a blessing. Can such people ever move past this hurt and pain and feel genuinely loved and accepted?

If you had asked Helen this question four years ago, her answer would have been an emphatic no. In her mind, the pain she had endured from an abusive father had forever trapped her in a cycle of insecurity, fear, and unrest. Many times she thought about a permanent way out of her pain. But she never had the courage to go through with it.

After years of anger, anxiety, and resentment, three years ago Helen discovered a way of escape. She began to understand and apply God's spiritual family blessing, something we will discover more about in this chapter.

Helen still struggles with her past at times, and those terrible pictures of nights of horror can still haunt her. Yet now she would answer the question "Is there any hope for those who received a curse from their parents?" with a resounding yes. She has hope in a God who was not willing to let a curse remain on her life. A God who has always provided help to people cursed by the crushing words or actions of others.

The Old Testament book of Deuteronomy has a verse that became an instant source of help for Helen. Like a buoy thrown to a drowning person, God's Word provided her with the encouragement to stay afloat until help arrived: "Nevertheless, the LORD your God would not listen to Balaam, *but the LORD your God turned the curse into a blessing* for you because the LORD your God loves you" (Deut. 23:5, italics added).

Let's learn a little more about the background and the important words that are found in this verse. This passage of Scripture can greatly minister to those who have come from a hurtful home.

Balaam was a sorcerer in the ancient Near East who was greatly respected by the pagan kings in the area. When the nation of Israel came up and camped just outside the Promised Land, this deeply worried one king named Balak. In fear and desperation, he sent for Balaam to come and curse God's people so that he could defeat them in battle.

The word *curse* is translated from the Hebrew word *qelalah*, which means "to esteem lightly, to dishonor."[1] (This word is used of a "scanty" meal or a thin "trickle" of water.) Something to be despised, something that was not of high value.

In Old Testament times, and even today, when we curse persons we devalue them. We take someone who is valuable and worthy of honor and blessing—like God's people in Balaam's time and each of His children today—and we place a value on them that is far below their actual worth.

God was not willing for that to happen to His people.

They were children of the mighty God who created the universe, and they carried high value because they were His. God took that curse of Balaam's and turned it into a blessing for His people instead. Let's see how this applies to someone struggling with a painful past, someone like Helen.

No one had to pay Helen's father to curse her. He seemed to enjoy making her life miserable. In fact, Helen would stay at school in the library or at a friend's house as long as she could before she had to go home. At least then maybe her father would have passed out from drinking too much. However, all too often he was awake and propped up in front of the television set when she came home. Then his "fun" would begin.

"Come over and give your father a hug," he would say when Helen tried to sneak past the living room door. She had no place to hide in her home. Her mother worked nights (and often didn't come home during the day), and Helen was left alone much of the time with her father. Without going into the tragic details, Helen was repeatedly subjected to the physical abuse of a sick father. Always careful that he didn't leave "marks that show on the outside," he was daily leaving heart-wrenching scars on Helen's inner life.

Spending so many evenings in the library to avoid her father paid an unexpected dividend to Helen. She graduated near the top of her class in high school and gladly accepted a scholarship to an out-of-state school.

However, physical distance does not equal emotional distance. Even though she was miles away in another state, Helen was still sitting next to her father emotionally.

Only after a number of years was Helen finally able to come to grips with her tragic past. She learned from a caring friend for the first time that God could take a curse from the past and turn it into a blessing.

What Helen learned about God's family blessing is what we would like to share with you in the remainder of this chapter. For the first time, she learned to be at home in the family of God when she accepted God's spiritual family blessing.

At Home with God's Family Blessing

Some children will never, in this life, hear words óf love or acceptance from their parents, people like Helen. Some will try to break down the door to their parents' hearts to receive this missing blessing, but all too often their attempt fails. For whatever reason, they have to face the fact that their blessing will have to come from another source.

When Helen finally realized this and turned to listen to the voice of her heavenly Father calling her, she discovered an open door of blessing. She found a spiritual family blessing that provided her with every element she had missed in her home.

"God's spiritual family blessing" begins with the fact that when we have a personal relationship with Jesus Christ, our spiritual parentage is secure.

AS BELIEVERS, OUR SPIRITUAL PARENTAGE IS SECURE

Helen was never secure in her relationship with her father. His anger had frozen within her heart a sense of insecurity. Yet when Helen trusted Jesus Christ as her Lord and Savior, she found out that she had a source of blessing that would be with her each day of her life and beyond! Helen discovered verses like these that speak of how stable her heavenly Father is and how permanent her relationship is with Him:

> "My sheep hear My voice, and I know them, and they follow Me; and I give them eternal life, and they shall never perish; neither shall anyone snatch them out of My hand" (John 10:27–28).
> And Jesus came and spoke to them, saying. . . . "lo, I am with you always, even to the end of the age" (Matt. 28:18, 20).
> For He Himself has said, "I will never desert you, nor will I ever forsake you," so that we confidently say, "The

Lord is my helper, I will not be afraid. What shall man do to me? (Heb. 13:5–6 NASB).

The Spirit of the Lord God is upon me, because the Lord has annointed me to bring good news to the afflicted; He has sent me to bind up the brokenhearted, to proclaim liberty to captives, and freedom to prisoners; . . . To comfort all who mourn, . . . giving them a garland instead of ashes, the oil of gladness instead of mourning, the mantle of praise instead of a spirit of fainting. So they will be called oaks of righteousness, the planting of the Lord, that He may be glorified (Isa. 61:1–3 NASB).

The first thing Helen had to consider when she came home at night was what kind of mood her father would be in. One night it would be anger, the next indifference; and occasionally he could even be very nice. His vacillations kept her so off balance, it left her insecure and questioning herself. Now she had a relationship with a heavenly Father characterized by the words, "He is the same yesterday, today, and forever" (Heb. 13:8 NASB).

Those who have personally believed in Jesus and trusted their lives to Him have a secure relationship with their heavenly Father. Yet there is even more to God's spiritual family blessing that they receive when they trust their lives to Him.

AS BELIEVERS, WE GAIN A SPIRITUAL FAMILY TO BLESS US

We began Chapter Three with the story about a little girl who was very scared and needed "someone with skin on" to hug her. As we saw in that chapter, our Lord knows all about our need for meaningful touch. He also knows our need for the physical companionship of others to build up our lives and encourage us.

That is why when we accept Christ, we gain not only a secure relationship with our heavenly Father, but we join an entire family of brothers and sisters in Christ! Men and women "with skin on" who can hug us and hold us and communicate God's love, wisdom, and blessing to us!

In many ways the early church provided a very good

model for us to follow. They were often in each other's homes (the earliest churches started in homes) and shared meals together. They were literally a family of the faith, and that is just how Paul expected Timothy to treat the believers he met. Listen to the counsel this noted apostle gave his young charge:

> Do not sharply rebuke an older man, but exhort him as a *father*, to the younger men as *brothers*, the older women as *mothers*, and the younger women as *sisters*, with all purity (1 Tim. 5:1–2 italics added).

Timothy was not related to these people by physical birth, but Paul points our clearly that he was related to them through spiritual birth. They all shared the same heavenly Father, and they were all necessary members of one another.

For both of the authors, this principle of having a spiritual family has been a tremendous personal help, particularly the way God used an older man in each of our lives to become a spiritual father to us in times of need.

Gary was in college when his father died, leaving a huge vacuum in his life. At this crossroads period in his life, a godly man named Rod Toews stepped in and became a spiritual father. Rod is a nationally prominent speaker and Christian educator. He could have easily let his busy schedule crowd out time for a hurting collegian. However, Rod attached high value to Gary and took him under his wing to shepherd and support. Both verbally and by his presence at a critical time, Rob gave Gary the blessing that was missing in his life now that his natural father had died.

John was a freshman in high school when he met a man who would become his spiritual father. Doug Barram, at the time a Young Life area director, had come to watch a freshman football game. Besides a few parents who were died-in-the-wool fans, *nobody* goes to freshman football games. Yet Doug was there, standing along the sidelines every game, offering words of encouragement to a young man who had not yet heard about Christ.

In the years that followed, this man took a fatherly interest in John and his two brothers. In a single-parent home, Doug added spiritual support to three boys who very much needed it. Each brother would come to know Jesus Christ and his Heavenly Father personally because of this man's deep love for his Savior, a love that was reflected in his fatherly love for them.

To return to Helen's story, she had a similar experience in learning how God's family can become that missing source of blessing she sought. Only hers came with a spiritual sister who blessed her at work.

Helen worked for a major oil company in the accounting department. One day, with the retirement of a woman at the office, Karen came to work. Karen was a committed Christian, who had prayed that God would provide the opportunity for her to share His love with someone who worked in her new office. That someone turned out to be Helen.

Karen was a mystery to Helen at first. She always seemed to have such a positive attitude and such a calm spirit even when there was great pressure at work. Perhaps more than anything Karen's lack of anxiety and inner peace drew Helen to want to be around her.

Soon, Karen and Helen had struck up a friendship and were sharing stories about the "rigors of dating" and their frustrations at work. But Karen also began sharing with Helen the good news about a heavenly Father Helen could come to know. At first, Helen didn't want anything to do with such talk. She had had enough of fathers to last a lifetime. Yet gradually, in spite of herself, the Holy Spirit working through Karen's life drew Helen to a saving knowledge of Christ.

Karen took Helen to church with her for the first time in Helen's adult life. Helen couldn't believe what happened. She was asked to stand up as a visitor, and she was greeted by the pastor. After church a number of people stopped her to say they were glad she had come. One elderly lady even hugged her! Helen went with Karen to the singles Sunday school class. People shared prayer requests before a short message, and they actually held hands and prayed for each other.

Helen found people who had never laid eyes on her treating her like a sister and encouraging her to come back. For the first time, Helen had seen the source of blessing a church family could be, and God used that experience literally to change her life.

Any person who has missed out on all or a part of their parents' blessing can acquire a spiritual family of fathers, mothers, brothers, and sisters who can fill that void. With a personal relationship with a heavenly Father that is secure, and through a spiritual family that can offer warmth, love, and acceptance, every element of the blessing can be ours and overflowing.

FOR BELIEVERS, EACH ELEMENT OF THE BLESSING IS AVAILABLE TODAY

Just in case you have forgotten (or are one of those readers who begin a book in the middle!), let's review the five elements we saw that are a part of the blessing to see how we can give it to each other:

- Meaningful touching
- A spoken message
- Attaching high value
- Picturing a special future
- Active commitment to see the blessing come to pass

Karen provided each element of the blessing to Helen, and it brought Helen to the Savior and to His church. By introducing Helen to a loving group of friends at church, Karen was able to see her blessing multiplied as many people took an interest in Helen's life.

As we will see in more detail in a later chapter, God has equipped the church, the local body of believers, to provide each aspect of the blessing to people in need. Where churches are growing and thriving anywhere in the country, you will find a body of believers who are practicing these five elements of the blessing. These are also the churches that are drawing in the unsaved, not simply luring other believers away from the church down the street.

The past three years had brought tremendous changes for Helen. She had come from feeling isolated and alone to feeling truly blessed for the first time in her life. Helen could retire now in the shelter of her caring friends at church and forget all about the past, right? Not quite. Her life still needed to go full circle.

Helen had received God's blessing from others. Now she would need to become a source of blessing to others around her. People in the office and at her apartment building for the first time could be thought of in terms of what she could give, not just what she needed from them. Because her life was filled with God's blessing through His Spirit and His people, she could love and serve them without needing it to be returned in response.

Helen had eaten fully and had drunk deeply from the feast of life God had provided her in His blessing. However, one final thing was left for Helen to do if she truly wanted to be free from her past. She would need to be a source of blessing not only to her friends at church and work, but to her enemies as well and to one enemy in particular.

GIVING THE BLESSING TO OTHERS—
EVEN OUR ENEMIES

As incredible as it may seem, Helen needed to become a source of blessing to her father, the very one who had caused her so much pain and had caused her to begin her search for acceptance in the first place.

"Couldn't I just skip over this part?" Helen asked her pastor when she found out her need to bless her father. Yet in her heart of hearts she knew she would never be truly free of his grip over her life until she could do this.

In a later chapter we will discover the way Helen went about re-establishing contact with her father and how she approached their first meeting in years. Suffice it to say that in spite of her change in attitude about blessing her father (which went from adamant refusal, to quiet aquiescence, to firm resolve, to wanting to chicken out at the last minute and not get on the plane to go see him), it was the second most meaningful day in her life.

Her most meaningful day was when she met the Lord Jesus, the One who changed her life by meeting her missing need for the blessing. He gave her a spiritual family to bless her in the present and provided her the power to be truly free from the yoke of the past.

Jesus is the Person who can change our life, or the life of loved ones who are struggling without the blessing, by providing us and them with God's spiritual family blessing. A blessing that not only parents need to give to their children, and vice versa, but one that can enrich your relationship with your spouse, intimate friends, and church family.

—11—

Giving the Blessing
to Your Spouse and Friends

Early in our research on this book, we went through this material with several couples in a Bible study group. We asked for the participants' honest evaluation of the material during the sessions, and then had them fill out a written evaluation at the end.

One of our favorite comments was written by a wife in the group. Commenting on what her husband had learned during the class, she wrote:

> Dennis has learned so much about how to "bless" the children. It has made a real difference in his relationship with them. How about teaching him how to bless me!!!

This woman's request was right on target. The elements of the blessing are not just limited to the parent/child relationship. We feel strongly that they can be found at the heart of *any* healthy relationship.

Let's continue to discover just how valuable applying the five elements of the blessing can be to three important relationships besides those with our children. First we will look at how the blessing can and should be given to a spouse and the relationship gains that can happen as a result. Then we will look at how friendships can be strengthened and developed through applying these same elements. Finally, in the next chapter, we will look at what can happen when a church family begins to apply these blessing principles to reach out to those beyond the church and especially to those within.

Being a Source of Blessing to Your Spouse

Laura was fed up with her husband and with all the upheaval in their lives. He often traveled out of town, and when he was home, he drank and made life miserable for her.

In her frustration, Laura came within an eyelash of throwing in the towel and filing for divorce, but her good friend Gayle talked her into going to see her pastor who she felt might be able to help. Even though Laura was reluctant at first, she was at the end of her rope. Against her better judgment, she made an appointment and went to see him.

For nearly forty minutes this wise pastor simply listened to her story. After Laura had shared her nonstop description of every one of her husband's faults, she finally sat back with a loud "Humph." Smugly she waited to hear an "Amen" from the pastor or at least a hearty confirmation that hers was the worst husband he had ever heard about.

At first the pastor didn't say a word. Deeply engrossed in thought, he literally waited several minutes before he spoke. Finally he sat up, looked her in the eye, and said gently, "Laura, have you ever forgiven your husband for all his many faults?"

You could have heard a pin drop. Laura had not expected to receive this kind of advice. ("No wonder his counseling is free," she thought.) Of course she had not forgiven her husband! He had never asked her to, and she wasn't about to bring it up. He had caused her to suffer, and she wasn't going to let him off the hook that easily.

"Laura, would you think about what I've said today, and would you promise to come back and see me next week?" As she grabbed her purse and headed for the door, she heard herself mutter something like "That would be fine, Pastor"; but she never thought she would be seeing him again. Yet something happened that week that began to change Laura's perspective on her marriage. Something drew her back to this man's office the next week.

In spite of telling herself repeatedly that she should simply forget what he had said, Laura did a great deal of thinking during the week. While it didn't all make sense, it began to dawn on her that it wasn't her husband who was on the hook—she was! He didn't lose any sleep about his behavior; she was the one getting ulcers.

Laura was still confused and had a great many questions for the pastor the next time they met. However, God had already begun to do some miraculous things in Laura's life. That afternoon, in the quietness of the pastor's study, she surrendered her life to Christ. She also decided to give up her need for revenge, to forgive her husband for all he had done, and to learn to love him unconditionally.

Laura's husband was a truck driver, and almost a week went by before he returned home. When he came into the house, he could have sworn he was at the wrong address. He couldn't believe how peaceful things were. Just a week ago everything he did made his wife mad; now she was going out of her way to do things for him.

When this rowdy truck driver found out Laura's change of heart had something to do with religion, he tossed her behavior aside as though it were another diet his wife had discovered. While it made things a lot nicer in the short run, soon her will power would fade away and they would be back at each other's throats.

After five months, Laura's *husband* made an appointment to see the same pastor she had seen. "You've got to tell me about what happened to Laura," the truck driver said. "She's changed so much. It's made me realize what a rotten husband I've been these past years. Pastor, I have a drinking problem, and I need help with it."

What made all the difference for this couple was that

Laura, in spite of the fact her husband didn't "deserve" it, decided to give him the blessing. For years she had made just the opposite decision. She had devalued him and even cursed him to his face. She hated his occupation that took him out of town and filled his clothes with the smell of diesel fuel.

When Laura's life was changed by the Source of blessing Himself, she was able out of the overflow of her life to attach high value to her husband and bless him. Instead of riding him about getting another job, she found ways to build him up and encourage him. Where once she had gone days without speaking to him when she was angry, now she told him her feeling, but without anger and hate. Meaningful touching even began to come back into their relationship, something that Laura had withheld from her husband when her spirit was unforgiving and bitter. As a result, her husband became so convicted about his behavior at home that he also made an appointment to see the pastor.

Granted, this is a dramatic example of what can happen when one spouse decides to be a source of blessing to the other. Their problems were of the major league variety and they needed to make a great deal of changes. However, in everyday households all across the country, with everyday problems and tensions, providing the elements of the blessing to a spouse can revive, encourage, and rejuvenate a marriage.

Let's look briefly at each element of the blessing and see just how important they can be to a healthy marriage. In fact, show us a couple that is growing together, and we'll show you two people practicing these principles of blessing.

MEANINGFUL TOUCH IN MARRIAGE

The same need for meaningful touching we saw with our children is equally important in a marriage. One wise husband realized the importance of this need during a difficult time for his wife, and it did more to minister to her than anything else he could have done.

When Marilyn was getting dressed one morning, she noticed something that didn't seem quite right. She noticed a small lump on her breast that she had not been aware of before.

Marilyn wasn't overly concerned, but she knew enough from reading magazines and watching television to know that she needed to get it checked. She told her husband, Art, what she intended to do, and then called the doctor for an appointment.

Two weeks later, Marilyn went to the doctor to have a biopsy done on the lump. Three days after her appointment, she was lying in a hospital bed facing a radical mastectomy. Besides coming to the hospital twice to deliver their two boys, this was the first time in her forty-seven years Marilyn had had to undergo an operation.

For Marilyn, the hardest thing she faced after the surgery wasn't her recovery, but what Art would think of her now. Would she still be attractive to him? How would he feel about touching her? Questions like these ran over and over in her mind.

The morning she was to be released from the hospital, Marilyn and Art were alone in her room. Her husband sat on her bed and took her hands in his. "Sugar," he said. "I want you to know something. You're as beautiful to me now as you were on our wedding night. Don't you ever forget that." Then Art looked over to make sure the door was shut, winked at her, and said, "After you get home and get rested up, we're going to have to get the lock fixed on the door."

Marilyn hugged her husband, and tears came to her eyes. She knew exactly what he meant by that last statement. Early in their marriage, when someone had forgotten to lock the door, one of the boys had walked into their room at a most inappropriate time. The result was that a new lock was installed on the door the next day, and a new saying began for them. "We're going to have to get the lock fixed on the door" became their private password to an intimate evening.

What had concerned Marilyn was not only how her operation would affect their sexual relationship, but whether it would keep Art from touching her outside the bedroom. His words and actions that morning assured her that this important element of the blessing would still be a part of their relationship.

Sexual touching is important in any growing relationship; however, it should not be the only time a couple touches. Dr. Kevin Lehman notes this in his book, *Sex Begins in the Kitchen*. He points out that genuine intimacy is developed in the small acts of touching in the kitchen, or walking through a mall together hand in hand, or sitting close together on the sofa watching television.

Speaking of "sex beginning in the kitchen," we heard a true story from a recent participant in a seminar who tried to apply the concept of meaningful touching with his wife, and it left him in an embarrassing situation!

After hearing the concept of meaningful touching talked about over and over, it really stuck with this man. One afternoon after cutting the grass, he came in to take a shower and clean up. He had left the bedroom door open and when he finished his shower he walked over to the rack to get a towel. From where he stood, he could see his wife standing in the kitchen preparing their dinner.

What a time for meaningful touching, he thought to himself. Without a moment's thought, he ran down the hall in his birthday suit and burst into the kitchen to give his wife a big hug. What he couldn't see from the bedroom or as he raced down the hall was his neighbor's wife who had come over to visit. That shocked neighbor saw a great deal more of this husband than she had ever expected! His timing was terrible, but no one could fault his commitment to meaningfully touch his wife!

Wise husbands and wives will include meaningful touching in their relationship with their spouse. It is the first part of giving the blessing.

A SPOKEN MESSAGE ATTACHING
HIGH VALUE TO A SPOUSE

Let's combine the next two elements of the blessing into one way of making sure your spouse receives the blessing. When we decide to place high value on our spouse, and then back that up with spoken words to that effect, it can do wonders for a relationship.

Using a word picture to praise a character trait of our children or our spouse is something we spent several pages discussing in Chapter Five. Like that royal couple we looked at in the Song of Solomon, husbands and wives can take on that look of royalty when they hear how highly we value them with our words.

A popular bumper sticker slogan reads, "Have you hugged your kids today?" Another, equally important phrase that you can copy and paste to your refrigerator, bathroom mirror, or forehead is:

Have You Praised
Your Mate
Today?

An everyday dose of praise, whether in the form of a word picture or just a statement like "Great dinner, Honey" or a "You are so kind to other people" or even a "You make me so proud the way you handle the children" can do wonders in a relationship.

Spoken words that attach high value to our spouse are so powerful that they can enrich almost any marriage. Why not try a project in your home to discover just how true this statement can be.

For one month, thirty days, praise at least one thing you appreciate about your spouse each day. Be sure you point out things about his or her character (being kind, generous, thoughtful, punctual, organized, and so on), as well as what they accomplish. Don't tell your husband or wife you're doing this. We give this assignment to many couples in counseling, and it in itself has caused positive changes in relationships.

While we have talked exclusively about using word pictures to praise a husband or wife, they can also be used to help discuss an important issue or avoid a heated argument. By using a word picture to convey a concern we have, instead of lashing out with damaging words, we can often motivate our mate to change and get across a message we can't seem to get across with only words.

One woman at a conference Gary was leading had a concern she had unsuccessfully tried to communicate to her husband for years. Yet by using a single word picture, she so affected him that he was willing to write her a $150,000 check right on the spot to build her dream house!

When we were talking through this story for the book, we kiddingly talked about asking people to mail in a dollar with a stamped self-addressed envelope to find out the word picture she used. We'd be rich in no time! We're sure every wife in America would like to know what she did to motivate her husband to respond the way he did.

You'll be glad to know that at absolutely no extra charge, we have decided to go ahead and tell you the word picture she used. Actually this story is not just about how one woman got her dream house. It is a beautiful example of how attaching high value to a spouse (in this case, not wanting to de-value a spouse in any way) can be powerfully communicated through a word picture.

Don and Bee are dear friends who have attended several relationship seminars that our ministry, Today's Family, has put on. As part of these seminars, Gary teaches couples and singles how to use word pictures with their spouse, their children, or in any meaningful relationship.

Bee had been struggling with something in her marriage for quite a long time. Something that ate away at her self-confidence and caused her constant embarrassment over the years. She was bothered about the condition of their house.

The Lord had greatly prospered Don's business, and much of their resources went into supporting their church and various ministries. They were both generous with their time as well. Don especially was always inviting a new couple at church home to dinner or offering to put up this missionary or that speaker.

Bee was every bit as hospitable, but she was the one having to struggle in an undersized kitchen to feed all the guests, or skip taking a shower because the hot-water heater allowed only three hot showers, or somehow finding a place for six or even ten people to sleep when there were only two beds in the house.

It was not a question of finances that held Don back from moving into a larger home; rather it was his desire not to be ostentatious and flaunt what God had given them. Bee understood her husband's motives and made do with the situation as best she could.

When Gary came back to their city for a second time, they signed up immediately for the seminar as a "refresher" course. After listening again to Gary share about using word pictures to communicate a concern with her spouse, Bee decided she would share one with her husband to describe her feelings toward the home she was living in. That night, she did share with her husband, and here is the word picture she used.

"Don, I feel like you're the game warden who takes such good care of the trout in the waterways around our house. You help keep the streams and ponds clean, and even make sure that when the trout are spawning, they have help getting upstream.

"When we were first married, I felt like I was one of those trout in the stream. I could see you standing on the bank, and I longed for you to scoop me up in a net and take me to the stream by your house. Then one day you

did come for me with a net and gently picked me out of
the water. It was the happiest time of my life; but instead
of ending up in the little stream, you put me in an old,
rusty barrel filled with fresh water.

"For twenty-two years you've made sure I had plenty
of food and you've kept the water clean, but I long for the
day when you will pick me up in your net and put me in
that little stream by your house. Don, that's the way I feel
about living in this house. I feel like we're living in a
rusty barrel, and it makes it hard on me and the people
we have over to the house."

Bee's years of longing came to an end that night. She
had talked to her husband numerous times about this
subject and had even tried to share her feelings with him
about their living situation. Yet Don had never seemed to
understand how important it was to her, until she shared
this word picture with him.

Don loved his wife deeply and had attached high value
to her throughout their marriage. He did not want to de-
value her in any way, so when he finally understood
through this story how she really felt about their house,
he responded immediately. Don wrote her a check that
night to hire an architect to draw up the plans for a new
home, a home where she could enjoy having people over,
serve them better, and have a comfortable place for them
to stay.

We could write an entire book about the benefits and
specific technique of using word pictures, but we hope
by this story you can see their usefulness in a marriage.
Whether you use a word picture in praising your spouse
or in sharing a concern, it can be a helpful tool to communicate words of high value to your mate.

PROVIDING A SPECIAL FUTURE FOR YOUR SPOUSE

The other night my (John's) wife and I were watching
part of a comedy show on television that we thought was
funny. The scene was a forest meadow where an outdoor
wedding was taking place.

There in the clearing were the bride and her attendant,

and the best man alongside the bridegroom, who looked worried and out of place. The minister asked the bride to say her vows, which she had made up especially for this occasion. Unhesitatingly, she launched into goal after goal, commitment after commitment, and dream after dream she had for herself, her husband, and their marriage. In fact, she went on so long night fell in the forest.

When she finally finished, the exhausted minister turned to the groom and asked him to repeat the vows *he* made up. Looking around nervously, his only words to the minister were, "Well, I hope this works out!"

His vows were not the kind of words that a new bride could build a secure future on. They were funny all right, but they did not provide the kind of security a wife needs to know that she has a special future ahead of her.

In a marriage, our mate needs to know that he or she is a special part of our future. What's more, our spouse needs to know that the way we look at him or her today leaves room for positive change and growth in the future. Tod learned this lesson the hard way with his wife, Betty.

Betty was not the world's best house cleaner. Her home was not what you would call neat and clean before they had children, and with three little ones running around, she had nearly given up on their home ever being clean. Like what happens in many marriages, her husband, Tod, had a different temperament. He was incredibly neat and clean. Tod even kept his workshop, where he spent time on his hobbies, so clean a person could safely eat off the floor.

Tod was so frustrated with his wife's sloppy ways, he spent much of his time berating her for being a poor house cleaner. She would *always* be messy and could *never* change. Tod told her stories about how, in the future, their house would become so dirty that their grandchildren would catch incurable diseases and the County Health Department would come out and shut them down.

Not only was Tod not placing high value on his wife, he was helping to see that the very thing he sought to change became a lasting part of their future! By painting a picture of his wife with no window of hope or door for change, he literally boxed her in to viewing herself as the "world's messiest housekeeper" that he thought she was.

In a Sunday school class, Tod saw for the first time how his words of a negative future had hurt his wife, not helped her. He learned that he was effectively killing any motivation his wife did have to change. His words of a negative future were telling his wife that it was impossible for her ever to please him. So why should she bother trying?

Tod thought back on what he had said to his wife. The times she had tried to make a dent in the house cleaning chores, he had met her with a "Finally!" or a "Why can't you keep things like that all the time?" But then he began to change.

Tod started to praise small things Betty did and to put aside the criticism of her poor performance. He even began to change his picture of her future and their house to a positive one. Change is always slow to take root, but it can grow ten times faster in the soil of encouragement than in the hard, rocky soil of criticism.

By picturing a special future for his wife in this area and encouraging her for small accomplishments, a miracle began to happen. Even though the house is not up to Tod's workshop standards, no longer does he have to fight his way through the laundry in the washroom or fear going into a shower that has things growing in it.

Whether it is the fear of entertaining, the need to go on a diet, failing to discipline the children promptly, or keeping a messy house, we do not motivate our mate to change by picturing a negative future. Our mate needs to hear words that picture a special future in the same way our children do, positive words that provide our spouse the room to become all that God can help him or her to become.

ACTIVE COMMITMENT TO YOUR MATE

As we have discovered in earlier chapters, providing the individual elements of the blessing without the glue to hold them all together is not enough. That glue is our active commitment. In fact, this final element of the blessing is at the heart of "cleaving" in a marriage.

When the Scriptures tell us we are to "cleave" to our spouse (Gen. 2:24), the root word in Hebrew means "to cling, to be firmly attached."[1] It takes a firm decision to be committed to blessing your spouse, a decision that will not remain intact if you don't make room for your mate's fallibilty.

In the 1929 Rose Bowl game, Georgia Tech came to California to meet the mighty football team from the University of California. In that game, something happened that demonstrated how fallible even a star could be.

Roy Riegels was a starter and star athlete for California. He had performed admirably during the regular season and was expected to make a great contribution to the team that day. What actually happened was that Roy made a winning contribution to the *other* team!

In a brilliant defensive play late in the first half, Roy intercepted a pass, fought off several would-be tacklers, and headed for the end zone and a touchdown. What he didn't know was that in fighting off the tacklers, he had gotten turned around and he actually scored a safety for the other team! When the half ended, Georgia Tech had gone ahead of California because of Roy's touchdown, and they hung on to win by that margin.

At halftime, everyone was wondering the same thing. Would Roy's coach, Nibbs Price, yank him out of the game? When it came time to announce the starting lineup for the second half, Price called out Roy's name! This coach had watched Roy work hard all season, and he remained committed to him even when he made a major mistake.

Another football coach, at the University of Texas, made famous an old country saying. Darryl Royal was like Coach Price; he remained committed to his starters in the game, even if they were fumbling the ball or missing a tackle. The press constantly asked him about this, and his reply was always the same, "You dance with the one who brung ya"—not good English, but an excellent example of active commitment.

What these two coaches had, and what every man or woman owes his or her spouse, is the willingness to stay committed, even if the other person fumbles the ball. Amy did this, and it was the very thing her husband credits with saving his life.

Grant owned a manufacturing business that had done quite well. His business was small, but it found its niche in the marketplace and was growing by leaps and bounds. Borrowing against the property and expecting his profits to continue, Grant took out a large loan to expand the facilities. No sooner had construction begun on his new plant than a multinational manufacturing concern decided to go into competition with Grant's product.

With cash flow tight because of the huge interest payments on the loan, Grant did not have the resources to put more salesmen on the street. Neither could Grant lower the price on his product because of the profit margin needed to keep the business afloat.

In less than a year, Grant had literally gone from riches to rags. His competitor had undercut his prices drastically to get into the marketplace, and it literally drove Grant out of business. Saddled with unpaid employees, lawsuits from suppliers, and with the bank breathing down his neck, Grant had to shut down his plant and liquidate his equipment at a fraction of its actual worth. He even lost his home that had been collateral for the note and had to move into a small apartment. Perhaps the crowning blow came when he had to explain to his children at midyear that they would have to change from the private school they loved to public school.

Grant was not a believer at the time of his business's collapse, and he was devastated as he had never been before. He even contemplated suicide, but one thing held him back:

> "I didn't know the Lord at the time my business went under, and my whole world seemed to end. I would like to say it was the thought of my children that kept me from ending it all, but that wouldn't be true.
>
> "The one thing that kept me from it was Amy and the way she constantly believed in me and blessed me with her love. Listening to her pray for me at night and having her hold me and let me cry were what pulled me through. I tell everybody she saved my life "twice." The first time was when the business failed; the second was when she led me to Jesus Christ!"

Grant could no longer provide for his wife and family "in the manner to which they had become accustomed." Yet because of this loving wife, who based her blessing for her husband on active commitment instead of material possessions, their relationship remained strong and secure.

Every husband and wife will drop the ball and prove themselves fallible time and again. If we are to be people of blessing, our commitment will rest on our decision to love our spouse "in spite of." Our love must be the kind of love that motivated our heavenly Father to bless us with his Son, in spite of the fact we didn't deserve it and because He knew we needed that blessing so much in our lives.

The blessing can make a tremendous difference in marriage, but it takes work to pull these principles off the page and apply them with our spouse. Even so, we know you won't regret a minute of time you spend cultivating each of the elements in your home, especially when you see the harvest of love and happiness that can result.

Being a Source of Blessing to Your Friends

We constantly meet people who "wish they had a close friend." Many of those same people would not have to make that comment if they knew how to be a "close friend." We discovered in studying the blessing in the Scriptures that an important part of becoming a close friend is to apply each element of the blessing in a friendship.

In all the Scriptures, perhaps the most universally acknowledged model of a close friend is Jonathan. His relationship with David is a graduate course in what makes a lasting relationship. These two young men were not a likely pair to strike up a friendship.

Jonathan was the heir apparent to his father's throne. He was also a mighty warrior in his own right. He led Israel's armies in battle and even attacked twenty Philistines with only his armor carrier to back him up and defeated them all (1 Sam. 14:6–14).

David and Jonathan first met just after David had slain Goliath. With all the attention David was getting, Jonathan could have looked at David as an arch rival and enemy. Yet we are told in the Scriptures that "the soul of Jonathan was knit to the soul of David, and Jonathan loved him as his own soul" (1 Sam. 18:1).

One reason that their friendship was unique is that it was a friend-to-friend relationship that included, and models for us, every aspect of the blessing.

Without the fear that exists today among men of appearing like homosexuals, David and Jonathan demonstrated meaningful touching in their friendship. In their last meeting, Jonathan had to tell David it was no longer safe for him to be around his father, Saul. We read that they "kissed one another and wept together, but David more so" (1 Sam. 20:41).

While men giving each other a kiss and crying in each others arms is almost taboo in our culture, it was not considered strange in ancient Israel nor is it unusual in many foreign countries today. Friends in these cultures demonstrate their love for each other with a kiss or a hug.

A friend today will include meaningful touching in blessing his or her friend. Withholding a hug or even a handshake from a friend can freeze that relationship at a surface level.

In giving us another picture of what it means to be a close friend, Jonathan spoke of his appreciation for David and placed high value on him. Let's look back on Jonathan's actions toward David when they first met.

David certainly stole the spotlight on that day. Yet we are told that "Jonathan took off the robe that was on him and gave it to David, with his armor" (1 Sam. 18:4). A warrior only lays down his weapons in front of someone he considers his better. Jonathan placed such high value on David that he was willing to sacrifice his symbols of authority (his armor and his robes) in order to honor his friend.

Jonathan also made a verbal covenant with David that he would be his close companion for life (1 Sam. 20:13). He said to David, "The LORD be with you as He has been with my father." No words of blessing were spared in what Jonathan said to David.

The last words Jonathan spoke to David illustrate his active commitment to David and his desire that God bless David in the future. "May the LORD be between you and me, and between my descendants and your descendants, forever" (1 Sam. 20:42).

Who are your true friends? Just think a moment about someone in your life who has been an intimate friend. Almost without exception, a close friend will be someone like Jonathan, a man or woman who has demonstrated each aspect of the blessing in his or her relationship with you. A close friend will be someone like Larry, who decided to provide each element of the blessing to his boss, Glenn.

Glenn was not an easy person to befriend. For one thing, Glenn didn't seem to *need* any friends. He was a tremendously successful businessman who always seemed on top of everything. Also, Glenn had been trained in the old tradition of maintaining professional distance from his employees and competitors. "Don't let anyone get close" was the unspoken motto Glenn lived by, that is, until the day his teenage son was picked up for selling illegal drugs to his classmates.

In order not to be taken advantage of by others, Glenn had built a wall around himself at work and at his church. He was constantly around people, yet he had no close friends. Glenn didn't even know how to be a friend to his wife or children, and the rebelliousness of his son and Glenn's total ignorance of his son's drug problem graphically pointed that out to him.

Now, in a time of dire need, Glenn needed the emotional support of a man he could pour his heart out to; and no one was there. No one was there until Larry noticed that something seemed wrong with his boss and decided that Glenn needed a friend, in spite of his nonverbal language that said just the opposite.

Larry was already an accomplished "Jonathan." He knew the importance of supplying another person with the elements of the blessing, and he had a number of close friends. But befriending Glenn was a different matter. He was his boss, and besides, Glenn certainly did not look as if he wanted any company.

Day by day, watching Glenn suffer in silence, Larry became convinced that he needed to befriend him. Their friendship began one Tuesday morning when Larry gathered up his courage, walked into Glenn's office, and laid his hand on Glenn's shoulder.

"Hey, old buddy," Larry said, "you just don't seem to have been yourself for a while. I may be way out of line, and you can tell me so if you want, but you seem to be really hurting. I just want you to know that if you ever need somebody to talk to, I'm around." Larry expected to be dismissed with a curt rebuff, but instead Glenn didn't say a word. Finally, after a long pause, he looked up at Larry, close to tears, and said, "I'll remember that, Larry. Thanks a lot."

Larry thought that was the end of things when a few days went by without hearing from Glenn. However on Friday, his secretary gave him the message that Glenn wanted to have breakfast with him one day that next week.

During that meeting, Larry listened, and listened, and *listened* to Glenn pour out a heart full of hurt. Larry didn't try to lecture Glenn, nor did Larry try to lessen the emotions that were present by saying, "Well, it's not all that bad" or "You're a Christian, Glenn, just pray about it." When Larry heard Glenn share the heartbreak that only comes with dealing with a rebellious child, he cried with him. The only time Larry remembered saying more than a sentence or two was when he prayed a short prayer with Glenn in his car after their breakfast.

Over the next several months, Larry met every week with Glenn to listen, talk, and pray about Glenn's relationship with his son. Larry couldn't directly relate to Glenn's hurt (Larry's children were just entering grade school), but he could still shake Glenn's hand and let him know that day or night, he had a friend he could turn to.

An interesting thing began to happen around the office as a result of Larry and Glenn's meeting. Glenn actually began to soften a little in his strict rule of professional distance. For the first time in years, Glenn had a friend who cared about him, and the result was that he was rediscovering how to be friends with others again.

Through Larry's providing each element of the blessing to his boss—by shaking his hand or patting Glenn on the back (meaningful touch); in speaking encouraging words to Glenn (spoken message); through pointing out the positive character traits that Glenn did have and the way he was trying to make a fresh start with his wife and the other children at home (attaching high value); by providing him with the hope of a special future that God could bring to pass regardless of how his son responded (special future); and by committing himself to be available to his friend when he needed someone to talk to (active commitment)—these two men's hearts began to be knitted together.

Things finally did get better with Glenn's son and as a result Glenn had *two* things to thank the Lord for. One was the new way his son responded to him as he began to become a better friend to him, and the other was an employee named Larry who had taught Glenn about genuine friendship by modeling for him the elements of the blessing.

Understanding the relationship elements of the blessing can communicate parental acceptance to a child, enrich a marriage, and deepen a friendship. But that is not all. The blessing can also provide helpful guidelines for a church family to use in remaining or becoming a place of blessing. Both to those outside the church and especially to those within.

— 12 —

A Church That Gives the Blessing

*J*im had struggled in his marriage, in his job as a mechanic, and in his life in general for many years. The only time he went to church was when he and his wife attended a wedding or when he was forced to attend an occasional Christmas or Easter service.

From Jim's perspective, the most encouraging place of fellowship he knew of was at the bowling alley with his Wednesday night bowling league. Jim lived for Wednesday nights when he and some of the guys from work would arrive early, have a few beers, and then bowl in league play.

From the slaps on the back for making a strike, to the closeness and camaraderie of being on a team, Jim looked at bowling as a shelter to get away from the storm clouds at work and the problems with his family. Unfortunately, after an evening at the lanes, Jim still had to go back home that night and to work the next day and face the reality that his life was falling apart all around him.

During the next year, through the example and loving commitment of a new mechanic at work, Jim heard the gospel for the first time. The new mechanic's name was Ed, and he was a deeply committed Christian. Jim quickly grew to respect Ed's skill in repairing engines, but it was his personal life that Jim envied even more. Ed was not perfect, but he had an inner peace and a growing marriage that Jim longed to have. Ed did not force his belief on Jim; rather he did something much more powerful. Ed lived a positive Christian life in front of his coworker, which was like giving salt to a thirsty man.

With Jim's marriage on the rocks and with his bordering on having a drinking problem, one afternoon Jim asked Ed why his life was so different from his (Jim's). Over the next several months, Ed met regularly with Jim and taught him about his need for the Savior and the new life he could have in Christ. On a cold day just before Christmas, Jim prayed with his friend Ed to receive Christ. After thirty-seven years of failing at life on his own, Jim finally turned to the Source of life Himself to lead him and guide him.

Like Jonathan in the Old Testament, Ed was a source of blessing to his friend. His personal caring helped Jim feel secure. Jim's personal life and his marriage began to change for the better as a result of God's working in his life. Ed also encouraged Jim to attend a church where he could learn more about God's Word.

Jim and his wife did begin to attend a fairly large church near their house. This church had an outstanding reputation as a Bible-believing church. However they never seemed to feel comfortable and accepted there. The preaching didn't bother Jim; in fact, he loved to learn from the pastor who was an excellent communicator. What hurt and confused him was the lack of personal relationships or warmth once the preaching was over.

Everyone was polite to Jim and his wife, but no one with bright eyes gave them a warm greeting, and dinner invitations after church were nonexistent. To try and develop some deeper friendships with other people at the church, they began attending a Sunday school class. However, after several months of attending the class, they were little closer to the people in the class than they were on the first Sunday they attended.

When Jim's friend Ed took a job at another auto shop out of state, Jim was crushed. He particularly ached over the lack of personal relationships with other men at the church. Since Jim had become a Christian, he had given up his Wednesday night bowling league to attend mid-week services. Yet without any committed Christian friends, he was getting lonelier and lonelier. Even when he tried to initiate a conversation with someone else at church, after an initial "Hi, how are you doing?" the strain to find topics to talk about would become uncomfortable. Finally Jim gave up trying at all. There were pockets of friendly people, but Jim noticed that they were friendly to the same people week after week.

This was Jim's first experience at a church and he began to feel that somehow Christians didn't need friends. He tried to immerse himself in studying the Bible and hoped that would take away his need for meaningful relationships. However, as time went by, Jim felt more alone when he was surrounded by the people at his church than he ever had at the bowling alley. The thought of switching churches never really occurred to Jim. This was the only church he had ever gone to and he felt certain this must be what they were all like.

With his only Christian friend gone and with no one at church that took a personal interest in his life, Jim began to spend more and more time with his old friends at work. As a result, he began to slip back into the old patterns he had before he became a Christian. Unfortunately, that included beginning to drink again.

Jim stopped attending Sunday school and attended only the church service. As the weeks went by, no one in his Sunday school class called to ask why he was no longer attending or even stopped him after church to say more than "Hello." While their lack of concern may have been from a feeling of "I didn't want to pry" or "We don't want to put pressure on him," in Jim's mind their indifference confirmed to him that they didn't care. Soon his attendance at the church service was sporadic.

With all the people at this growing church, no one seemed to miss one man who began drifting away from the fellowship; that is, until the pastor unexpectedly ran into Jim's wife one Saturday at the market.

"Hi," said the pastor. "How are you and Jim doing?" It was only an innocent question, but it was met with tears and sobs right in the middle of a supermarket aisle. "Pastor, Jim won't come back to church with me. He said that he has better friends at the bowling alley than he ever did at church."

Jim had been searching for closeness in relationships and a blessing from his church family, but he never found it. In less than ten months, Jim had gone from sitting at the midweek service at church to drinking beer again with his buddies back at the bowling alley. Perhaps Jim should have been mature enough to stay in the church and to concentrate on giving to others, never receiving love back himself, but he wasn't. And neither are many new believers just like Jim.

Is this simply the story of one man who had too little faith? We wish it were. Unfortunately this story can be told of many churches today that talk about the blessings of genuine fellowship (*koinonia*) in a sermon or in a Sunday school class, but do not practice it with people within the church. While we may not like to admit it in the evangelical community, many people who come to our churches find more of the elements of the blessing in a bowling alley than they do inside the church walls.

Instead of letting this discourage those of us inside the church, it should encourage us to learn how to be a people of blessing. We need to learn how to make significant relationships within the church, not superficial ones. From the first time God called a special people to be His own until today, we as believers have always been called to be a blessing to others.

Our Calling Is to Be a People of Blessing

From earliest times, God's people have been called to be a blessing. When God first came to Abraham, He gave him a very specific promise. We read: "I will bless you / And make your name great; / And you shall be a blessing. . . . In you shall all the families of the earth be blessed" (Gen. 12:2–3).

Centuries later, in the book of Acts, Peter tells us what form this blessing took for all nations. The blessing came in the body of the suffering servant, Jesus, a descendant of Abraham's who has the power to bless our lives by freeing us from sin. Peter said:

> "God . . . says to Abraham, 'Through your offspring all peoples on earth will be blessed.' When God raised up his servant, he sent Him first to you to bless you by turning each of you from your wicked ways" (3:25–26 NIV).

Introducing people to Jesus Christ is the first and foremost way a church can bless others. When men and women are introduced to the Source of blessing, they come face to face with Someone who can be their best friend and their very source of life.

If we have been called to provide people with the blessing of knowing Christ, what is the best way to see that happen? Let's let our Lord answer that question. "A new commandment I give to you, that you love one another. . . . All [people] will know that you are My disciples, if you have love for one another" (John 13:34–35). What does that mean to us?

People outside the church will never care how much we know about Christ until they know how much we care for each other. When a body of believers becomes committed to loving each other, then they can truly be called a church that is serious about winning others to Christ.

The Blessing: A Churchwide Guideline for Loving Others

If Jesus commanded us to be people who deeply love each other, why do so many churches struggle with being warm and sensitive to the needs of others? Is it a lack of loving people in the church?

We fully believe that it is not the lack of caring believers in the church that results in people like Jim going away unblessed. Rather, these people lack the knowledge about how they can practically meet the relational needs other people have once they come to know Christ.

The church needs to be first and foremost a place where the gospel is preached and where Christ is honored as our Lord and Savior. But God designed the church to be a caring community as well. We can't escape the fact that when we fail to bless and love our brothers and sisters in Christ, we are failing in our duties as a family of God. When one member of the body rejoices, we should all rejoice. When one member weeps, we should all weep (1 Cor. 12:26).

The exciting thing about the concept of the blessing is that it can be a guideline for all kinds of loving relationships. Obviously it can provide a tangible way for parents to bless their children. We have also seen how a marriage and even an intimate friendship can be built up by the elements of the blessing. However, it doesn't stop there. Some churches today train and encourage their people to provide each aspect of the blessing to others. And thankfully more and more churches are learning to do this training.

In fact, show us a church anywhere in the world that is meeting the genuine needs of its members and drawing others to Christ, and we'll show you a church where God's Word is being taught and where the relationship elements of the blessing are being applied.

What happens when a church, or even a department within a church, gets hold of the concept of the blessing?

Let's look at how the principles of the blessing, applied in one church's singles department, literally turned their ministry around.

A Case Study of Applying the Blessing with God's People

Mark was the leader of a large singles Sunday school class. In fact, on any given Sunday, they could have more than 150 young men and women in attendance. Like many church groups, Mark's class struggled with the problems of turnover and building depth relationships. They had the heart for ministry to others, but that caring desire never seemed to move out of their class leaders' meetings and into their class.

Almost two years ago, we shared the principles in this book at a conference Mark attended. He jumped on every bit of information we could give him about the blessing and asked us to speak at a class retreat he had coming up. God used that conference Mark attended and the ensuing class retreat to plant the biblical principles of the blessing within the hearts of the people in the class.

We found out only a few months ago that after the retreat, Mark formed a group of people within the class called the Blessing Bunch. Their goal was to identify people in the class who particularly needed one or more elements of the blessing and then actively to commit themselves to be the person that provided that need.

With one young lady in the class who had broken an engagement, providing the blessing meant simply taking her hands and crying with her. For a man, it involved a brother in Christ picturing a special future for him that gave him the confidence to tackle a difficult new assignment. Still another woman needed to know she was of high value to her friend and to the Lord after a week of listening to her employer say she was worthless.

Having a strategy for meeting needs within the group by teaching and applying the elements of the blessing became a real help to this leader. In fact, Mark talked about the principles of blessing so much, many of the class members would say to each other in fun, "Have you had your blessing this week?"

"Have you had your blessing this week?" These people meant this as a joke, yet making the people in that class aware of the elements of the blessing opened many doors of ministry, doors to a number of men's and women's lives that had once been tightly closed. But what happened in this singles group did not stay confined to their classroom. Giving the blessing began to spread throughout the entire church.

Several of the members of the class became convicted about their relationships with their parents as they learned about the concept of the blessing. One young man in particular walked out of the classroom one Sunday morning and right to a pay phone where he called his father for the first time in more than four years. Other people began to share the principles of the blessing with their family members at the church and it too led to a time of healing.

The singles class even talked about the concept of the blessing at a Sunday evening service a few weeks following their retreat. One thing Mark shared was that the married people in the church could bless the singles by not expecting them to get married tomorrow and by inviting them into their homes. This began an "adopt a single" program that helped bring a once nearly isolated group into the mainstream of church life.

This story is of just one department that decided to get serious about blessing other people in their lives. The results spread throughout the entire church and helped bring a new sense of warmth and caring to many people.

Imagine what would happen if an entire church decided to bless those in their fellowship and were trained how to do it! We would have a church where relationship needs were actively being met by a welcoming handshake or hug (meaningful touch); where appreciation for a fine sermon, working in the childrens department, or simply listening to a hurting brother or sister was verbally acknowledged (spoken message). We would have groups of believers who acknowledged every member's true worth (attaching high value) and who gave them words of hope and encouragement to reach their God-given potential (a special future). All these elements would be wrapped in the willingness to let people fail and not let them walk away unnoticed, because a decision had been made already that they were valuable (an active commitment).

This church sounds like the kind of church most of us would like to belong to, and it can be. All it takes is one person to start a Blessing Bunch to begin to meet the needs of those around them. Even more than that, this kind of church can become the kind of place that those outside the church long to be a part of, a true place of blessing.

A church that is committed to applying the principles of the blessing can make a tremendous impact on the unsaved. Once church members learn about this concept and experience it within the church, they can begin to transport it outside the church walls. Monday through Saturday they can provide the elements of God's blessing to a non-Christian society desperately in search of genuine security and acceptance.

An employer can evaluate how well he or she is doing in being a blessing to his or her employees. A school teacher can learn about the blessing and recognize the tell-tale signs of a child's growing up without parental acceptance. A student can befriend a fellow classmate and point him or her toward a secure source of blessing through Christ.

Hitting the Target When It Comes to Loving Each Other

Aristotle once observed, "You stand a far greater chance of hitting the target if you can see it." At first glance, this statement might not sound too profound, but it really is. Churches, parents, spouses, and friends stand a far better chance of hitting the target of loving each other if they can see how to do it.

Following the guidelines provided in the blessing can help our words and actions score a bull's-eye when we want to communicate God's love and acceptance to our loved ones. Coupled with sound teaching from the Word of God, the elements of the blessing can also provide a tremendous tool for evangelism. The blessing can even help us fulfill the Great Commission to "Go and make disciples of all nations" (Matt. 28:19). If the mark of disciples is that they "love one another" (John 13:35), applying the principles of the blessing can help God's love radiate to a needy world.

As we end our look at how the blessing applies to our church family, we are nearing the end of our journey in this book. However, we have one more important stop to make. There are two people in our lives who can especially profit from a blessing we can give them—our parents.

Before we look at how we as children can give back a blessing to our parents, let's listen to the words of a song that capture the kind of place the church needs to be: a shelter for those who have faced the storms of life, and a place where God's love radiates to a needy world; a place where the blessing is given to others and where authenticity is a password to fellowship. A place Ken Medema pictures in these haunting words:[1]

If This Is Not A Place . . .

If this is not a place, where tears are understood,
  then where shall I go to cry?
And if this is not a place, where my spirit can take
  wings, then where shall I go to fly?*

I don't need another place, for trying to impress you,
  with just how good and virtuous I am.
No, no, no, I don't need another place, for always
  being on top of things. Everybody knows that it's a
  sham, it's a sham.

I don't need another place for always wearing smiles,
  even when it's not the way I feel.
I don't need another place, to mouth the same old
  platitudes; everybody knows that it's not real.

So if this is not a place, where my questions can be
  asked, then where shall I go to seek?
And if this is not a place, where my heart cry can be
  heard, where, tell me where, shall I go to speak?

So if this is not a place, where tears are understood,
  where shall I go, where shall I go to fly?*

—13—

Giving the Blessing to Your Parents

*O*ur portrait of the blessing is almost complete. In past chapters we have used broad strokes to illustrate how the blessing was viewed down through the centuries. We have also used the fine strokes of the literal meaning of the word *blessing* to bring out the subtle nuances of this concept. Five predominant patterns run throughout the painting, each an important element of the blessing, and together they provide the viewer with a sense of structure and balance. Stories of people, past and present, have been used to bring color and depth to the picture. Some of these colors are dark and subdued and stir our compassion. These are the stories of Esau and others like him who never received their family's blessing. Yet we have also tried to paint the brilliant colors of joy, happiness, and security from the lives of those who have received the blessing.

However, before we lay down our brush and move away from this portrait of the blessing, we need to paint one final corner. In fact, this corner is a key to completing our picture and truly capturing its total scope.

In our final strokes to complete this portrait of the blessing, we need to illustrate the importance of seeing the blessing go full circle. We began painting in a corner of the canvas that showed how parents need to give their children the blessing; we will end by seeing how these same children need to return the blessing to their parents. Helen returned the blessing, even though it was the most difficult thing she had ever done in her life.

A Story of Blessing

Let's look back at the story of Helen. Helen had been physically abused by her father the entire time she was growing up. He was an alcoholic whose changing moods left her insecure, fearful, and distressed. The first chance Helen had to leave home, she was out the door. From her perspective, she didn't care if she ever saw her father again, an attitude that was confirmed when he and her mother were divorced while she was in college. Helen had absolutely no reason to go home now and refused even to consider the thought.

Then Helen met a co-worker named Karen, and her whole life began to change. For the first time, she heard about and received God's blessing of salvation and His provision of a spiritual family at church to help meet her needs. With spiritual fathers galore at her church, Helen felt even less of a need to make peace with her natural father.

Gradually, Helen began to notice that some areas of her spiritual life were lagging behind. She had grown by leaps and bounds, but still had a tendency to criticize others. She had come a long way, but her temper still needed control. For a long time, Helen thought these nagging tendencies did not disappear because of a lack of faith or knowledge of God's Word. Countless times she had committed herself afresh to study God's Word. Yet her struggles continued.

Then one day Helen discovered what was at the heart of her problem. She did not lack faith; she was not willing to honor her father. The deep bitterness and resentment she felt still had an iron grip on part of her life, an area she had not opened up to God's leadership, healing, and love.

When Helen looked closely at her life, she found she was becoming more and more like the person she hated most in life—her father. Until and unless she dealt with the stranglehold he still held on her life, she would find a continuing struggle in her spiritual life and possible destruction in her personal relationships.

At first, Helen tried to push away the growing conviction that she needed to deal with her relationship with her father. Even thinking about him again hurt her. This is always the case when we remember something painful from the past. Memories bring back with them feelings, and sometimes those feelings are the things we don't want to face. However Helen knew what was right. While her emotions didn't agree, she knew that God honored those who honored their parents. By remaining at enmity with her father, she was doing what was wrong and was draining herself of life.

Helen went to see her pastor and explained what God had been showing her over the past several months. After several sessions of prayer and counsel, Helen decided to visit her father. Whether he would respond or not, she was determined to bless and honor him.

On June 14, sitting in the pastor's study, Helen made the most difficult call of her life. She had found out her father's phone number from an old family friend and, after praying with her pastor, picked up the phone and dialed the out-of-state number.

She made the call at 3:00 P.M., and secretly Helen hoped her father would be at work and not be there to answer the phone. But on the fifth ring, her father answered the phone. God gave Helen the strength to choke out, "Hello, Dad?" After a long silence on the other end, he replied, "Helen?"

In a short conversation, Helen told her father she was going to be flying to his city and asked if she could see him. "Please do, Helen," her father said. She got directions to his apartment and hung up the phone.

The first skirmish had been won, but the battle still lay before her. A hundred times in the four days before her flight Helen talked herself in and out of going to see her father. Yet each time she decided to back out, that still, small voice within her convicted her of what was right. If she received nothing from her father except the pain she had gotten in the past, she knew she still needed to go for *her* sake and do what was right.

Helen did board the plane, and her pastor and several friends came with her to the airport to encourage her and see her off. The flight was both the shortest and longest airplane flight of her life. Helen rented a car when she arrived at the airport and drove the thirty minutes to her father's home. With a deep sigh and a short prayer, Helen walked to his apartment and knocked on the door.

An old, tired-looking man opened the door. (Why had she remembered him as being such a giant?) Sitting on the couch with her father, Helen poured out her heart to him. She told about becoming a Christian and the difference it had made in her life. Then, hardest of all, she admitted the anger and hatred she had carried toward him for years and asked his forgiveness.

By the time Helen finished talking, they were both in tears. For fifteen years Helen's father had denied the burning conviction of his wrongs against his daughter. He asked her to forgive him for being such a terrible father and lamented over all the pain he had caused in her life.

After four hours that seemed like only four minutes, Helen left. At the door she put her arms around her father and heard herself say the words that she never thought she could say: "I love you, Daddy." All the hurt he had caused in her life had not stopped her from loving him. Even during the times when she hated him the most, she still felt an attachment to him and a love for the man who had brought her into the world. Where once she could not express that love or even feel it, now she felt compassion, pity, and warmth for a man who had shattered his own life when he shattered hers.

Helen went back to her home, her office, and her church a new person. Not looking different on the outside, but knowing that on the inside she was more free than she had ever been in her life.

When she had come to know Christ, He had freed her from the guilt of every sin and unlocked the shackles that kept her chained to the past. By having the courage to face her father, to honor and bless him, Helen finally took off the shackles Christ had unlocked. She walked away from her father's house that day free to truly live in the present, because she was at last unchained from the past.

The First Commandment with a Promise

What Helen was willing to do in facing her father took a tremendous amount of courage. However, Helen had a God who understood her fears and gave her the strength to face them.

Is it only those like Helen, who have such a hurtful past, who need to bless their parents? Certainly not. In fact, the Scriptures direct every child to give the blessing to his or her parents.

In the book of Ephesians, Paul goes into detail about what it means to have healthy family relationships. In the fifth chapter of this book he gives a beautiful picture of God's design for the husband/wife relationship. With the man as a loving leader and the woman as a highly valued partner and responder, the stage is set for children to come into a loving home.

Paul's next instructions are for those children. While under the roof and protection of one's parents, children are to "obey your parents in the Lord" (Eph. 6:1). Then Paul gives a general admonition for children of all ages: "Honor your father and mother, which is the first commandment with a promise: that it may be well with you, and you may live long on the earth" (Eph. 6:2–3).

What does it mean to honor your parents? We can see that if we will look at the word *honor* in the Scriptures. In Hebrew, the word for "honor" is *kabed*. This word literally means, "to be heavy, weighty, to honor."[1] Even today, we still link the idea of being heavy with honoring a person.

When the President of the United States or some other important person speaks, people often say that his words "carry a lot of weight." Someone whose words are weighty is someone worthy of honor and respect. However, we can learn even more about what it means to honor someone by looking at its opposite in the Scriptures.

In Chapter Ten, we discovered that the literal meaning of the word *curse, (qalal)* was "to make light, of little weight, to dishonor."[2] If we go back to our example above, if we dishonor a person we would say, "Their words carry little weight." The contrast is striking!

When Paul tells us to honor our parents, he is telling us that they are worthy of high value and respect. In modern-day terms, we could call them a heavyweight in our lives! Just the opposite is true if we choose to dishonor our parents.

Some people treat their parents as if they are a layer of dust on a table. Dust weighs almost nothing and can be swept away with a brush of the hand. Dust is a nuisance and an eyesore that clouds any real beauty the table might have. Paul tells us that such an attitude should not be a part of how any child views his or her parents, and for good reason. If we fail to honor our parents, we not only do what is wrong and dishonor God, but we also literally drain ourselves of life!

What Happens When You Honor (or Dishonor) Your Parents?

Paul goes on to remind us in this passage in Ephesians that a promise is available to all those who will keep the commandment to honor their parents. However, we need to understand something about the promises of God before we look any further. The first thing to remember is that God's promises are always fulfilled. What God promises, He will see come to pass.

The second striking reality we need to see about this promise is that it is conditional. If you fulfill the conditions of the promise, God will honor that in your life. God's promise to you cuts both ways. If you will honor your parents, this promise will apply. But if you dishonor them, you will have to live life apart from God's promise.

Paul tells us that two aspects to this promise relate to those who would honor their parents. The first reflects on our relationship with God.

"THAT IT MAY GO WELL WITH YOU"

In New Testament Greek, this entire phrase is captured in the tiny word, *eu*. In ancient Greece, this word was used to salute someone with the words, "Well done! Excellent!"[3] When you honor your parents, the first thing you can know for sure is that God is saying to you, "Well done! Excellent!"

For God's people, doing what was right before God has always included doing what was right by their parents. In Leviticus 19:3, Moses commands the people, "Every one of you shall revere his mother and father, and keep My Sabbaths: I am the LORD your God." Linked with the importance of setting aside a special Sabbath day each week to honor God is the command to be consistent in reverencing and honoring your parents.

Jesus felt just as strongly that the actions you take toward your parents reflect your heart toward God. If you are dishonoring your parents, you are following the tradition of your times, not the Word of God. Listen to the strong rebuke Jesus gave the Pharisees and scribes who willfully chose to dishonor their parents:

> "Why do you also transgress the commandment of God because of your tradition? For God commanded, saying, 'Honor your father and mother.' . . . But you say, 'Whoever says to his father or mother, "Whatever profit you might have received from me has been dedicated to the temple" is released from honoring his father or mother.' . . . Hypocrites! Well did Isaiah prophesy about you saying:

> 'These people draw near to Me with
>   their mouth,
> And honor Me with their lips,
> But their heart is far from Me' " (Matt. 15:3–8).

For Jesus, doing what was wrong in dishonoring your parents could never be linked with what was right in God's eyes. Anyone who urges you to dishonor your parents speaks words of hypocrisy and falsehood. You will only hear a "well done" from your heavenly Father when you honor your parents, not if you dishonor them by treating them as a speck of dust.

Not only does it affect your relationship with the Lord when you follow what is right in honoring your parents, God promises that it will affect your own life in a positive way as well!

"THAT YOU MAY LIVE LONG ON THE EARTH"

God promises that those who will honor their parents actually receive life! How can this be? Just ask many physicians, counselors, or pastors. They have seen in their offices the shattered lives of those who dishonor their parents, with their strength drained away as a result.

Each of you has only so much emotional and physical energy, and you choose how you will spend it. What physicians and researchers are finding out more and more clearly today is that a close link exists between what we think and how we physically react.

Positive attitudes have been linked with positive physiological changes while negative attitudes can open the door for illness or disease.[4] When persons choose to hate or dishonor their parents because of anger, bitterness, or resentment, they pay a spiritual, emotional, and physical price.

The Scriptures have shown the strong connection between the words we speak and how they affect us physically. In Proverbs 16:24 we read, "Pleasant words are like a honeycomb, sweetness to the soul and health to the bones," and in a later passage, "A merry heart does good, like medicine,/But a broken spirit dries the bones" (Prov. 17:22).

When you decide to honor your parents, you are placing high value on them. God says such actions will increase your life on the earth. However, if you decide to see your life dried up by holding on to bitterness or resentment toward your parents (attitudes of dishonor), you eat up your strength and shorten your very life.

Some people have been dishonoring their parents for years. If that is something you have been doing through your actions or attitudes, you need to deal with it as soon as possible and begin the process of making things right. Otherwise the words of King David can ring true in your life, "When I kept silent about my sin, my body wasted away/Through my groaning all day long./For day and night, Thy hand was heavy upon me;/My vitality was drained away as with the fever-heat of summer" (Ps. 32:3–4 NASB).

Paul's words have clearly demonstrated to us that we need to honor our parents. Yet, practically, how do we do this? Once again, we find ourselves at the doorstep of the blessing.

How Do You Honor Your Parents?

The book of Proverbs was written to teach us the skill of right living. We have already seen that honoring your parents is the right thing to do, but how is it done? You honor your parents by acting as wise people, not as fools.

Many of the Proverbs talk about and illustrate different kinds of fools. All are people who are not applying God's principles for right living. One vivid description of a destructive fool is found near the end of the book. Look at this description of a worthless, treacherous man. Then go back and see what heads the list of things that characterize him:

> There is a kind of man who curses his father,
> And does not bless his mother.
> There is a kind who is pure in his own eyes,

Yet is not washed from his filthiness.
There is a kind—oh, how lofty are his eyes!
And their eyelids are raised in arrogance.
There is a kind of man whose teeth are like swords,
And his jaw teeth like knives (Prov. 30:11–14 NASB).

The man pictured above brings pain to those at home and those outside the home. As we have already seen, he also robs himself of life by cursing his parents. However, he is not only being rebuked in this passage for cursing them, he is also being scolded because he did not bless them.

If you want to be a person who honors your parents, you will be a person who blesses them. In providing the blessing to your parents, you truly honor them, do what is right in God's eyes, and even prolong your life.

We have talked at length in earlier chapters about the five elements of the blessing. We have seen these elements applied to our children, our spouse, our friends, and our church family. Yet where these elements can be of tremendous importance is in providing a blessing for our parents. Each one can be a useful tool in honoring them.

To begin with, your parents need you to *meaningfully touch* them. Even if they have struggled with hugging and touching you when you were young, as they grow older they need the reassurance that comes from being touched.

They also need *spoken words* from their children. Isn't it interesting that Mother's Day is the busiest day of the year for interstate phone calls! For many mothers, these will be the only encouraging words they hear from their children until the next year. Unfortunately, many fathers will hear fewer words of praise. You need to be consistent in your contact with your parents. They need to hear your voice and the spoken words of blessing they carry.

It is common for a parent to think back in guilt on the past. The things that often seem to stand out to a parent are not the many positive things they did, but the times they spoke out in anger or did something that accidentally hurt their child. When you bless your parents with words that *attach high value* to them, you can be a tremendous encouragement in their lives. You do not have to pretend a wrong was never committed, but you can forgive them and keep them from self-pity. You can decide to value them highly, to honor them because of the great worth they have to you and to God.

Parents need words that picture a *special future* for them. In fact, for many parents the reason they can only look back to times past is because they do not feel a sense of a future in their lives. You can point out useful and beneficial aspects to your parents' lives, even if those useful qualities are different than when they were younger. You can also point them to the Scriptures and the encouragement that their future with their heavenly Father and spiritual family does not end when this life does.

Something that can help is assuring your parents of their important place in the family as the years go by. In some homes with older parents, the grown children will take over the finances and all major decisions and toss aside an older parent's advice or input. Nothing is wrong with providing a helpful service to your parents, but you should be sure you still honor them in the process. By continuing to ask for their wisdom and advice, you can provide them with a picture of a special future.

One last thing that can encourage a special future for your parents is letting them be a part of your future, the future wrapped up in your children. Providing the time for grandparents and grandchildren to meet and interact can be a tremendous tool for providing your parents with a special future. If you will let them know how they can be and have been a blessing to your children, you honor them in a very valuable way.

Of all the ways you can bless your parents, the genuine commitment to walk with your parents through each step in life is particularly important at the end of their lives. Particularly when one parent dies, the other will need an extra measure of your love and commitment to lean on in his or her journey through life.

"But You Never Met My Parents!"

We know this chapter will be the hardest one for some people to read in the entire book. Already someone may be saying to himself, "Bless *my* parents? Are you kidding? After what they did to me? After what they put me through? That's easy for Smalley and Trent to say. *They never met my parents!*"

Is it really possible to honor *any* parent? Aren't some fathers or mothers—people like Helen's father—so cruel or hurtful to their children that they don't deserve blessing?

We don't deny for a moment that there are parents who, from a human perspective, do not deserve a blessing. Often in our counseling sessions we hear stories of a father or mother for whom a cold shoulder would be far more appropriate than warm words. However, as much as we may long for an exception clause, we can't mistake the clear command of Scripture that we "honor our mother and father."

Let's be clear what we're saying. Making a decision to honor our parents does not mean that we allow our alcoholic father to put our children in the car and drive them across the city. Neither does it mean that we call our verbally abusive mother once a day, when each call is an invitation to further attack. However, it does mean that we make a decision to attach value to them and not to dishonor them in spite of their alcoholism or temper.

In part, that's why we've taken several chapters in our book *The Gift of Honor* to specifically talk about what it means to honor our parents. We point out that when we dishonor mom and dad, we, not they, are the ones who sustain the most damage. Not only that, but we also share how experiencing trials in a hurtful home can be something we learn to use to build up our worth rather than lower it.

Honoring a Parent's Memory

Throughout this chapter, we have challenged you to bless and honor your parents and make peace with your past. However, we know that some readers' parents have already died. What about them? What happens when you can't talk face to face with your parents and speak words of blessing to them? What if Helen's father had died before she had the chance to talk with him?

For you to truly release a parent who has died, you need to deal with your memory of that person. The memory of an absent mother or father can often be just as vivid as real life.

Each of you carries mental pictures of lost loved ones that you can call to mind. For some of you who loved your parents deeply but never really told them so, honoring a parent's memory is one way of blessing them. For others who struggle with a painful past, as you talk with your Lord about your negative feelings toward them, you can find the kind of freedom that Helen found in facing up to her father.

If this is your situation, let us make a few suggestions. First, try writing a letter to that person describing what you would share with him or her if she or he were with you in person. If writing is difficult, make a cassette tape that you can play back and listen to. Remember we are called to honor our parents, not tear up their memory with hateful words. You can still be painfully honest, and yet not sin with your words.

Being free to be a person of blessing means having dealt honestly with the past. If you have only the memory of your parents rather than their physical presence, you can still honor them and make things right between the Lord and your memory of them.

Coming Full Circle with the Blessing

In honoring our parents as very valuable, we have come full circle in our look at how the blessing in the

Scriptures can enrich and encourage healthy relationships. Many of us have never thought in terms of providing our parents with the blessing. But if we will, we can leave them a tangible gift of love that they can carry throughout their lives, just as Don and his brother and sisters did for their parents.

Cindy and I (John) have been to some very creative parties over the years. From "re"gressive dinners to "Roaring Twenties" nights, we thought we had seen them all. Then an invitation came that really caught our attention. We were being asked to attend a surprise, "This Is Your Life" party for an older couple in our church.

The party had been planned by the children in this family specifically to honor their parents for years of loving care and sacrifice. It wasn't anybody's birthday, nor was it tied in with an anniversary. It was simply an evening to remember and say thank you for years of commitment to friends and family.

There was not a dry eye in the place by the time the evening was finished. Thanks to the oldest son's, Don's, initiative, their parents had received an evening of blessing from their children. As we left this older couple's house, you could see in their eyes that their hearts were bursting with pride, appreciation, and love. These children had provided their parents with an evening that was worth far more to them than any department store gift from their children ever could be.

Please don't assume that "my parents would never let us do something like that for them." If Don's parents had known what was coming, they would have probably tried to talk their children out of the evening. Yet regardless of how difficult it can be for some parents to let their children give back to them, we need to make an effort to bless them. In Appendix A at the end of this book, we have included suggestions on how to plan a special evening of blessing for those you love. Has it been too long since you honored your parents with words of blessing? All you need is an active commitment to give back to them what God has already richly given you.

—14—

A Final Blessing

~~~

We hope that discovering more about the blessing in the Scriptures has challenged each of you to have a new reason and a new way to honor your parents, your children, your spouse, your friends, and your church family. Our prayer for each reader is that your life will be one where each element of the blessing is given and received.

Remember, we build the blessing into a person's life on a daily basis. You never know what small act of love and encouragement will be the one that your children, spouse, or friends remember as a key way in which you blessed them. How do we know this? In seminars throughout the country and in numerous counseling sessions with couples and individuals, we asked people this question: "What is one specific way you knew that you had received your parents' blessing?" Let's look at how one hundred people responded to this question. Through their responses we can discover how powerful a parent's everyday actions and attitudes are in communicating the blessing to their children.

One Hundred Homes That Gave the Blessing to Children

1. *My parents would take the time to really listen to me when I talked to them by looking directly into my eyes.*

2. We were often spontaneously getting hugged even apart from completing a task or chore.

3. They would let me explain my side of the story.

4. We went camping as a family. *(This response was repeated often.)*

5. They would take each of us out individually for a special breakfast with Mom and Dad.

6. My father would put his arm around me at church and let me lay my head on his shoulder.

7. I got to spend one day at Dad's office, seeing where he worked and meeting the people he worked with.

8. My mother always carried pictures of each of us in her purse.

9. They would watch their tone of voice when they argued.

10. My parents made sure that each one of us kids appeared in the family photos.

11. My parents would make a special Christmas ornament for each child that represented a character trait we had worked on that year.

12. They were willing to admit when they were wrong and say "I'm sorry."

13. They had a "king or queen for a day meal" for us that would focus individual attention on each child.

14. As a family we often read and discussed the book The Velveteen Rabbit, *which talks about how valuable we are.*

15. I saw my parents praying for me even when I didn't feel I deserved it.

16. My folks wrote up a special "story of my birth" that they read to me every year.

17. We read Psalm 139 as a family and discussed how God had uniquely and specially designed each of us children.

18. *They attended all of my open houses at school.*

19. *My father loved me by loving my mother.*

20. *They would tell us character traits we possessed that would help us be a good marriage partner when we grew up and got married.*

21. *My mother would tell us "make believe" bedtime stories that illustrated positive character traits she felt we had.*

22. *They tried to be consistent in disciplining me.*

23. *My mom was always willing to help me with my math homework.*

24. *My folks really tried to help me think through where I should go to college.*

25. *My dad would constantly tell me that whoever I married, he'd be committed to him and our children for life.*

26. *My parents openly discussed and helped me set limits in the sexual area.*

27. *My mother and father would ask us children our opinions on important family decisions.*

28. *When my father was facing being transferred at work, he purposely took another job so that I could finish my senior year in high school at the same school.*

29. *My mom had a great sense of humor, but she never made us kids the brunt of her jokes.*

30. *My parents wouldn't change things in my bedroom without asking me if it were OK with me.*

31. *My folks pursued resolving conflict with me instead of letting issues build up.*

32. *When I wrecked my parents' car, my father's first reaction was to hug me and let me cry instead of yelling at me.*

33. *My dad could correct me without getting all emotional or lecturing me.*

34. *My parents were patient with me when I went through my long hair stage in high school.*

35. *My mother tried really hard to keep her promises to me.*

36. *My dad would ask me all the time, "What would it take for this to be a 'great year' for you?" and then try to see that it was.*

37. *Even though my dad had played football in college, he never forced me to go out for sports when I didn't want to.*

38. *At least once a year around my birthday, my dad would take me out of school for a special lunch where he would let me know I was special to him.*

39. *My parents would tell me over and over that I was a good friend to my friends.*

40. *Even when I was in high school, my father sometimes would tuck me into bed like when I was little.*

41. *My mother would pray with me about important decisions I was facing, or even that I would have a good day at school.*

42. *When I was thirteen, my dad trusted me to use his favorite hunting rifle when I was invited to go hunting with a friend and his father.*

43. *We would have "family meetings" every two weeks where everyone would share their goals and problems.*

44. *If it was really cold, my mom would get up early and drive me on my paper route.*

45. *When I had my appendix out, my parents were right there with me before and after the operation.*

46. *Sometimes when I would get home from school, my mother would have left a plate of cookies on the counter with a special note saying she loved me.*

47. *My parents used to take me and a friend out for a special dinner sometimes.*

48. *When I had a teacher that didn't like me, my parents defended me and stood up for me.*

49. *My mother got interested in computers just because I was interested in them.*

50. *They could have just shipped my stuff, but my parents drove a U-Haul trailer over 1,800 miles when I went off to college.*

51. *My dad gave up smoking because he knew how much it bothered Mom and us kids.*

52. *My father taught me how to budget my money.*

53. *Even though I didn't like it at the time, the chores my parents made me do helped me learn responsibility.*

54. *My parents would always make sure I knew why I was being disciplined.*

55. *My father let me go with him on some of his business trips.*

56. *I realize now how hard my mother worked to take care of us all.*

57. *My parents were good examples to me of how a Christian marriage should function.*

58. *When I was down about my boyfriend breaking up with me, my father took extra time just to listen to me and cry with me.*

59. *My parents never acted like they were perfect, and they never expected us to be perfect either.*

60. *Now that I'm an adult, I really appreciate how my father taught me to communicate with him. That has helped me know how to talk to my husband now that I'm married.*

61. *My mother would let me explain my point of view on issues—even when she disagreed with me. She always made me feel that my opinion was important.*

62. *My parents didn't compare my abilities with those*

of my older brother or the other kids at school, but helped me see my own unique value.

63. *My parents allowed me to give back to them when I got older, like picking up the tab at dinner.*

64. *I appreciated my father working to keep a good relationship with me when I was a teenager. I can see now that helped keep me from some really bad dating relationships.*

65. *When I asked for it, my mother would give me advice on dating and other areas of my life.*

66. *I always had the best sack lunch at school of anybody in my class.*

67. *My folks were always willing to hang in there with me and help me work through conflicts with my friends.*

68. *My father went with me when I had to take back an ugly dress a saleswoman had talked me into buying.*

69. *My mother was always interested in what I was doing at school, but she wasn't interfering.*

70. *My father acted more excited about getting to spend time with us kids than he did about working at the office.*

71. *My father helped me buy an old Mustang that had been wrecked and worked with me to rebuild it into a beautiful car.*

72. *I never felt like I had to perform to gain my father's approval.*

73. *My father worked with me for hours on my soap-box derby racer.*

74. *Some people's parents criticize them behind their backs, but I was always hearing something positive from my parents' friends that my parents had said about me.*

75. *My mother had a Bible study with me every Monday morning before I went to school.*

76. *Even though I didn't appreciate it at the time, I know that my parents were protecting me by putting a curfew on when I had to be in on a date.*

77. *When I first started wearing make-up, my mother never made fun of how much time I spent in front of the mirror.*

78. *Even when I was very overweight in high school, my parents still made me feel I was attractive.*

79. *My mom took on a part-time job to help me earn enough money to go to a Christian summer camp.*

80. *My parents paid for me to take several vocational tests when I was struggling to find out what I wanted to do for a living.*

81. *My father would reward me for a job well done on the yard by taking me to Dairy Queen where we would both get a sundae.*

82. *My father let me share in his failures as well as his successes.*

83. *My father went with me to six different used car dealers to help me find my first car.*

84. *My parents would always make sure that each of us children was introduced to their friends when they came over to our house.*

85. *My parents quit using a "nickname" that really hurt me.*

86. *My mom used to rub my legs after cheerleader practice.*

87. *My father would always point out my good table manners to others.*

88. *My mother would see to it that I had the necessary tools to complete a project (crayons, ruler, and so on).*

89. *My father would put a special note on our pillows when he had to go out of town on business.*

90. *My parents would involve the whole family in planning family vacations.*

91. *My father took me and my sisters out on a very special date on our sixteenth birthdays.*

92. *They would always go to my piano recitals and act interested.*

93. *My father would let me practice pitching to him for a long time when he got home from work.*

94. *We used a special red plate at dinner to designate birthdays or outstanding achievements.*

95. *Every Saturday morning, my father would get up before anybody else and cook us all pancakes and bacon.*

96. *We always went out to eat as a family after church and discussed what we had learned at Sunday school.*

97. *My father would ask to talk to each of us kids personally when he called in from a trip.*

98. *We would all hold hands together when we said grace; then when we finished, we would squeeze the person's hand next to us three times, which stood for the three words, "I love you."*

99. *My mother would slow down when I helped her cook to let us accomplish the task together.*

100. *Even though I had never seen him cry before, my father cried during my wedding because he was going to miss me no longer being at home.*

Sounds like a lot of small things, doesn't it? Yet these small acts of love and acceptance left a lasting impression on these people's hearts. Each act was actually a decision a parent made to provide an element of the blessing to a child. A blessing that even now, years later, is remembered and cherished.

We could have included a list of "one hundred ways to bless your spouse, friends, or church family," but we're sure you get the idea. Providing the blessing to those we love can encourage and enrich their lives. It also does wonders for the one giving the blessing as well. We have looked at the children of one hundred families who provided the elements of the blessing to their children. Our prayer is that your family will become number one hundred and one.

A Personal Message

As we close this book and our look at the blessing, we hope you've been encouraged and challenged to be a person of blessing. But we don't want to leave you with just our thoughts on these pages. We would also like to leave you with our blessing for your life.

If we could reach out to each of you reading this book right now, and place our hands on your shoulder, our final blessing to you would be the words of Aaron, in the Old Testament (Num. 6:24–26).

May God enable you to become a mighty source of blessing, and may these words always ring true in your life:

"The Lord bless you and keep you;

The Lord make His face to shine upon you, and be gracious to you;

The Lord lift up His countenance upon you, and give you peace."

Gary Smalley   John Trent

—Appendix A—

Evenings of Blessing
to Apply with Your Loved Ones

It's good to talk or read about the blessing, but putting its elements into practice is even better. That's why we want to give you four sample "Evenings of Blessing" that you can adapt and use with your loved ones.

What follows are suggestions we have either tried ourselves or know have been successful with other people or groups. The best way to use them is to take ideas from the sample evenings that follow and add your own special touches. (Then write us at Today's Family, P.O. Box 22111, Phoenix, AZ 85028, and tell us the ways of blessing you've come up with and how your evening went. We're always looking for new ways to bless people and would love to hear yours.)

None of these ideas is sacred. One husband actually had a "Morning of Blessing" instead of an "Evening of Blessing" for his wife that included breakfast in bed. Be creative and have fun. Most of all, know that you can waste precious time on a thousand different things, but you will never waste one minute in blessing your loved ones.

An Evening of Blessing for Your Children

Goal: That your children will know and experience your love for them in a special setting and in a unique way.

Basic Idea: Whether this evening happens once or several times a year, each child in the family would have a time when he or she experiences the elements of the blessing from his or her parents (or parent in a single-parent home).

Possible Program: We know several people who have tied their time of blessing in with a birthday celebration. Again, feel free to vary these suggestions so that they bless your uniquely special child.

1. Give your child(ren) several days' notice that this evening is coming. Half the fun for children is anticipating an event, particularly when it involves a special time for them!

2. Ask your child ahead of time what his or her favorite meal would be and use that as your guide for a festive dinner to begin the evening. Be prepared for peanut butter and hot dogs as a main course, topped off with chocolate cake for dessert (and then Rolaids on the side). Remember, this is your opportunity to honor them. That doesn't mean that you can't sneak in a vegetable or something nutritious, but it should be a meal your child feels is fit for that "king" or "queen" in your household.

3. Beginning with holding hands when you say grace at the meal, meaningful touching or hugging should be a part of this time of blessing.

4. You can bless your children with a spoken message in several ways, attaching high value to them and providing them with the picture of a special future. Here are a few things you could try after dinner.

- Put together a slide show or picture album showing each year of the child's life that you have on film.
- Each parent can list five to ten things about that child that the parent has appreciated over the past year. (Try to pick character traits as well as accomplishments.)
- Each parent could also say a word about how these character traits will help the son or daughter be a godly, helpful, or loving person in the years to come.
- Pick out an everyday object and use it as a word pic-

ture to share a praise with your child, or to point out
a talent God could use in the future. One dad we
know used a sponge to picture his son! "Henry," he
said, "this past year you've reminded me of a
sponge. You've soaked up your Sunday school lessons like a sponge and then squeezed out big drops
of love all over your little brothers and sister and
your mom and me."

• Present your child with a homemade gift. This isn't
the time for an early Christmas present. Make sure if
you do give a gift it's something that your finger-
prints are all over. One mother we know gave her
daughter a beautiful afghan she had spent months
working on that became the beginning of her daughter's hope chest.

• Some parents like to write out a "story of their
child's birth" and read it to their child. This story
talks about the special events of the nine months before birth, their mad dash to the hospital, and the
indescribable joy of seeing their little one for the
first time. It blesses children to know that they were
planned and looked forward to (regardless of
whether they came in our timing or not).

5. While it can be short, take the time to formally
bless and pray for your child. (Be sure to look at Appendix B to see several sample blessings based on scriptural
passages you may want to use.)

• Sing a hymn or a familiar chorus as a way of transi-
tion from slides or a fun story.

• Candles fascinate children (and many adults). The
lighting of candles is an important part of blessing
children in orthodox Jewish homes, and it's something you might want to try. This act can also be a
good way to get the other children in the family involved.

• If your denomination permits, sharing Communion
with older children is especially meaningful. This
can also be a time to ask forgiveness if we have of-
fended anyone in the family and a chance to focus

together on the cup of blessing that represents Christ's love for us.

• Write out a few short sentences for you to read that express your love and appreciation for your child. This would be a special time to lay your hand on the child's shoulder or head while you bless him or her. Whether as a prayer, or with eyes open, your words can be something like the simple blessing below. Here's an example of a blessing for a boy named Joseph. (Again, look in Appendix B for other examples based on scriptural passages.)

"Thank You, Lord, for our son, Joseph. We ask that You be the source of his joy and the Source of his life. Help us as parents to love Joseph as You would have us love him. Thank You for the way he is already growing into the unique person You designed him to be. Lord, we know how special Joseph is to You, and tonight may he realize how valuable he is to us now and forever. May he become all You intend him to be, and we are honored that we are his parents. Bless us all now, for it's in Jesus' name we pray."

Closing Comments: Again, these are just a few suggestions on how you could design an evening of blessing for your children. For some children, ending the evening with a special family activity or even a VCR movie they have picked out would be a "10" to them. Others may just want to talk to you or have a hug. However you design this evening, it can be a special and meaningful time for you and your children.

An Evening of Blessing for Your Spouse

Goal: To set aside a meaningful time to provide your husband or wife with each of the elements of the blessing.

Basic Idea: Plan an evening for your spouse that will be a memorable time as he or she experiences your love and high value for him or her. While this evening can adopt some of the same elements that were a part of blessing a child, you can personalize this time for a husband or wife in several ways.

Possible Program: An anniversary is always a good time to provide a spouse with an evening of blessing. However, any evening apart from the children and away from the phone will do.

1. If there is money available, you might want to consider going to a hotel room for the night. Many nice hotels and resorts have special weekend rates when their weekday business guests are gone. If money is tight, why not try swapping houses with a close friend for one night. This means that you trade houses with another couple for one night (leaving your kids for them to babysit) and agree to swap with them at some future date. Swapping houses cuts the cost way down and still lets you have the privacy to really focus on each other.

2. As with the times of blessing in the Scriptures, a special meal is always a great way to start things off. Remember to include your spouse's favorite dish. Even if you have a coupon for a steak dinner, if he or she would rather have fish, honor that request.

3. You can communicate your love to your spouse by expressing your commitment to your marriage and by pointing out several of your spouse's endearing qualities. Here are some practical ways to do that:

- Write a "story of our marriage" where you recapture some of the drama and excitement of your courtship and of each season of your marriage. If you're not a writer, try making a tape recording of your fond memories. While talking into a microphone may seem a little awkward at first, this can leave a lasting record for your spouse of some of the things you appreciate about him or her.
- Photographs of special times together can be very endearing. Pictures bring back memories and memories bring back feelings. Just looking again at a few happy times you have shared together (without go-

ing overboard and showing ten trays of slides of your one fishing trip together) can do wonders to set a positive tone for the evening.

- Select one or several everyday objects to use as a word picture to communicate things you appreciate about your spouse. One husband used a bottle of "White Out" correcting fluid as a word picture to praise his wife. "Sweetheart," he said, "you remind me of this little bottle of 'White Out.' Every time I make a mistake or do something to hurt you, you cover over my faults with your love like covering mistakes on a page. Every day with you, I get to start with a clean sheet of paper." Don't underestimate the power of such pictures! As we have stressed before, word pictures can leave a lasting positive impression on your spouse.
- One way to picture a special future for your spouse is to dig out your original wedding vows and repeat them. Something else that is special is to write a new set of vows that expresses your love and commitment. If you did not memorize and repeat your own set of vows during your wedding, here's your chance to do it!

  Appendix B can give you some good ideas that you can apply to blessing your spouse.
- If your denomination permits, partaking in Communion as you re-commit your life to your spouse can be a beautiful and meaningful part of an evening of blessing.
- List ten reasons why, of all the guys or girls in the world, you would choose your spouse again to be your life-partner.
- Take an extended time to pray together, thanking God for each other and asking God to keep your love as fresh and refreshing as Spring.

4. Since you've gone to all the trouble to get away for the weekend, meaningful touching as a married couple can take on a whole new meaning after a special evening of sharing words of love and commitment.

An Evening for Children to Bless Their Parents

Goal: For children who have now grown up to take a special time to provide the elements of the blessing to their parents.

Basic Idea: Many parents are used to giving the elements of the blessing to their children, but they may not be as used to receiving them in return. In this evening, children have a chance to give back words of love and acceptance that they have received as a way of honoring their parents.

(If one parent has died or if your parents are divorced, do not avoid such an evening simply because it might remind the parent too much of the departed loved one. While we need to be sensitive, we can still honor a parent's memory who has died and provide needed words of love and encouragement to the parent who remains behind. If your parents are divorced, at another private time you could share a time of blessing with your other parent.)

Possible Program: You might want to turn to the end of Chapter Thirteen to see some of the ways Don and his brother and sisters designed a special evening of blessing for their parents. Each set of parents is different, and it can be difficult for some parents to receive these words of love from their children. However, time and time again we have heard that embarrassed or uncomfortable parents have warmed up to their children's words of blessing and then treasured them for the rest of their lives.

PLEASE NOTE: While grandchildren are special in and of themselves to their grandparents, for this one evening they should be left at home with a babysitter. Children are wonderful and delightful, but they can also be distracting. The children should have their special time of blessing. This should be a time to focus all our attention on our parents.

1. If possible, try to gather each brother and sister together for this time of blessing. If someone absolutely can't make it for some reason, get them to send a tape

recording of some words of blessing they can share with their parents. Why a tape? Listening to a person's voice has a way of putting them right in the room with you. Also, like taping the entire evening, it can give a parent a record of this missing child's thoughts.

2. What would an evening of blessing be without a special dinner! Parents like to eat too—especially if you cook some of their favorite items, and then forbid them to help clean up the dishes.

3. Slides or old family photo albums can be a tremendous tool for remembering fun times in the past as a family. Again, don't overdo it. Remember the words Jack Benny once said to a reporter who asked him, "What do you want to be remembered for?" Benny replied, "I would like to have carved on my tombstone, 'Here lies a man who never bored his friends with home movies!'" Pictures won't be boring to your parents, but be sensitive about how many you show.

4. Each child can then share five positive character traits that their parents built into their life. In other words, how are you a different person today because of the parents God has given you? Don and his brother and sisters shared in this way and it had an incredible impact. As you can tell, this activity will take some advance planning and careful thought on the part of each child. But the results will be well worth it.

5. Homemade gifts or a special portrait of the children might make a special gift for your parents at an evening of blessing.

6. Let's not forget how an everyday object used as a word picture can bring encouragement to your parents' hearts. One person we know told her mother, "Mom, when we were growing up, you reminded me of a fork. Your eyes were always sharp enough to catch us when we were doing something wrong, and you had more than one good point!" While you may not want to use a fork, we're sure at least twenty objects in the very room you're sitting in could be used to point out the high value of your parents.

7. A special time of prayer for our parents, with everyone gathered around them arm in arm, can be a memorable way to close such an evening. Don't expect this to be an emotionless time. While we can share love with each other by laughing together, it is also healing to cry together. This is not to say we should try to force any emotions, but rather allow both tears and laughter to be a part of the evening.

Closing Comments: Many people wait too long to share words of blessing with their parents, or they simply don't know how to do it. Armed with all the suggestions above, what's stopping you from honoring your parents with an evening of blessing? Forget about giving them an all-expense-paid trip to the Bahamas as a way of showing you love them. Expressing your love and appreciation for them is the best present you could ever give them. (But don't let them know you substituted their trip to the Bahamas for this time of blessing!)

An Evening of Blessing with Your Church Family

You say it has been too long since you had a church potluck dinner? Here's a special evening with your church family that can help you get to know new people, honor those who have served the Lord in a special way, and learn more about blessing God all in one!

Goal: To provide an evening when our church family can come together to bless each other and bless the Lord.

Basic Idea: Invite church families to a potluck dinner that centers around the theme of "blessing."

Possible Program: Talk about having fun while you're doing something meaningful. Watching a popular television program can't hold a candle to the excitement and light of God's love that can flow through a time when the church family is gathered to bless each other.

1. Ask each family to bring a main course to feed their own family, and then a dish to share that says something about their roots. For example, one family's origins might be Swedish and they could bring Swedish meat-

balls or fondue. Another family might be French and they could bring pastries or even French onion soup. If they are all-American "Jones," they can bring hot dogs or even apple pie. It they're not up on their ethnic roots, they could bring a dish that represents their geographical roots. For example, if one family is from Washington State, they could bring baked apples. Each family should label their dish as to its origins. Sharing a meal like this is a great way to get to know a little bit about the background of people in the church.[1]

2. As an admission ticket to get into the dinner, each adult should be required to bring a verse from the Bible that has been a blessing in his or her life. Just before grace is said, or later in the program, the pastor or program leader can randomly call on a table and have someone there share his or her favorite verse. Or each person could share his or her verse with the others at the table as a way to encourage each other and get to know each other better.

3. You will bless the children and parents who attend by providing child care for the little ones before the more serious part of the evening begins. After the meal would be a good time to have the little ones march out to a movie or to special games.

4. We are told in the Scriptures to bless the Lord. What better way to do so than with our church family and friends. Here are some ways this can happen during the evening program:

- Sing several songs in your hymnal that focus on the theme of God blessing us or our blessing Him. Hymns or choruses like "Make Me a Blessing" and "Bless the Lord, O My Soul" can be a meaningful way to bless our Lord with song.
- We are told to bless God's holy name. Ask the pastor or a church leader to talk briefly about the names of God in the Scriptures and how each name gives us a new reason to praise Him.
- Communion is a tremendous way for us to come face to face with God's priceless blessing in sacrificing

His Son for our sins. Even the Scriptures tell us that Communion is a "blessing." In 1 Corinthians 10:16 we read, "The cup of blessing which we bless, is it not the communion of the blood of Christ?" (KJV). In keeping with preparation for Communion, perhaps if someone in the congregation has dishonored someone else in some way, he or she can be encouraged to go to that person and ask his or her forgiveness to set things right.

- In some churches, a foot-washing service could be another way to bow the knee to our brother or sister in Christ by humbling ourselves to wash another's feet.
- One church had a large, blank poster at the front of the room. Each table had pencils, paper, and straight pins. After a short message on how faithful God had been in blessing the congregation over the years, the pastor asked people to write down one way in which God had blessed them over the past year. Then anyone who wanted could come up to the front, read or share how God had blessed them, and pin their paper on the blank poster. By the end of the evening, dozens of testimonies to God's gracious blessings were pinned to that poster.
- This time can even be used to bless other people in the church for a job well done or simply for being a good friend or godly example. You might even want to ask people to come prepared to share word pictures that illustrate traits they appreciate about another member of the congregation.
- Close the ceremony of blessing by holding hands and singing a closing chorus or benediction. If the early church could greet each other with a holy hug and kiss, we should at least be able to take each other's hands as we close this time of blessing.

Can you imagine what would happen if parents, spouses, adult children, and even entire churches put these evenings of blessing into practice? So many people's lives would change for the better that it would drive us out of a job when it comes to marriage and family counseling. And we'd love it! We hope you'll adopt even one evening of blessing described above as a model for designing one of your own and that it will prove to be one of the most encouraging times in your loved one's and your own life.

—Appendix B—

Sample Blessings
Based on the Scriptures

*These are some ways that you can bless your children
or even your mate by inserting his or her name where
the blank is on each passage.*

"*H*ow blessed _____ will be because
you do not walk in the counsel of the wicked, nor stand in
the path of sinners, nor do you sit in the seat of scoffers.
But as your parents we have seen you delight in the law
of the Lord. You have been thinking about His law day
and night. May God make you, _____,
like a tree firmly planted by streams of water. May God
allow you to grow and bear His fruit in His season and
your life will not wither and whatever you shall do, it will
prosper!" (Psalm 1)

"O Lord may _____ always abide in
Thy love. May [he] dwell in Your holy presence. May [he]
walk with integrity and do works of righteousness. May
[he] speak truth in [his] heart and not slander with [his]
tongue nor do evil to [his] friends, nor get revenge on
[his] friends.

"May _____ despise being a repro-
bate and value those who honor You. May [he] always
keep [his] word for the good of others and not cheat [his]
friends or use their misfortune for [his] benefit, Nor take
bribes against the innocent. Consequently you Lord,

have promised that _____ will never be shaken." (Psalm 15)

"O Lord, may _____ come to know Your wisdom and instruction. May [he] discern the sayings of understanding, May [he] receive the instruction in wise behavior, righteousness, justice, and equity. May You Lord give [him] prudence, knowledge, and discretion. May [he] truly listen and increase in learning, always seeking wise counsel. May [he] come to understand the greatest of all Your instructions, to love and value You with all [his] heart. Then will [he] begin to know knowledge." (Proverbs 1)

"Lord, may _____ trust in You with all [his] heart and may [he] not lean on [his] own understanding. But may [he] seek to know what You would want [him] to do in all [he] does. Then You have promised to make [his] paths straight." (Proverbs 3:5–6)

"May _____ never try to be wise in [his] own eyes, but may [he] learn to value You above all else and keep turning away from evil ways and thinking.

"Then You have promised to heal [his] body and refresh [his] bones." (Proverbs 3:7–8)

"Lord, may _____ never lose the willingness to turn from reproof. Behold then You have promised to pour out Your spirit on [him] and to make Your words known to [him]! If [he] does not turn to Your ways You have also promised to refuse to listen to [his] cry or grab [his] hand in distress.

"May _____ never neglect Your counsel nor turn from Your counsel nor turn from Your reproof." (Proverbs 1:23–25)

"My [son or daughter] _____:
If you will:
• Receive and believe what God says

- Treasure with high value His commandments
- Listen attentively to His wisdom
- Draw your heart to understanding Him
- Cry out for discernment
- Raise your voice for understanding
- Seek Him more than silver or hidden treasures

"Then you, _____, will understand how to honor God.

"God will give you knowledge and wisdom. From Him you will receive understanding for God has been storing up wisdom for you because you have sought Him above all else.

"He will be your shield, your bodyguard, and He will preserve your way." (Proverbs 2:1–8)

"Oh Lord, may _____ never forget Your teaching. Let [his] heart keep Your commandments. Then Lord, You will give _____ many more days and years to [his] life and You will add peace to [his] life.

"May kindness and truth never leave [him]. Lord, may [he] bind them around [his] neck and write them on [his] heart.

"Then Lord, You will give [him] favor and a good reputation both with You and man." (Proverbs 3:1–4)

Notes

Chapter One

1. For an expanded description of what it means to "leave home," see the chapters "The Importance of 'Leaving' Home" and "Hard-to-Leave Homes" in the book *Growing Together,* by Dr. John Trent, Victor Books, 1985.

Chapter Two

1. Gleason L. Archer, Jr., *Old Testament Introduction* (Chicago: Moody Press, 1964), p. 223.

2. Francis Brown, S. R. Driver, and Charles A. Briggs, *A Hebrew and English Lexicon of the Old Testament* (Oxford: Clarendon Press, reprinted edition, 1974), p. 139.

3. David Hunt and T. A. McMahon, *The Seduction of Christianity* (Eugene, Ore.: Harvest House, 1985), pp. 28–29.

4. Nathan Ausbubel, *The Book of Jewish Knowledge* (New York: Crown Publishers, 1964), p. 98.

5. J. A. Thompson, *The Bible and Archaeology* (Grand Rapids: Wm. B. Eerdmans Publishing, 1972 edition), p. 26.

6. K. A. Kitchen, *Ancient Orient and Old Testament* (Chicago: Inter-Varsity Press, 1966), p. 154.

7. C. H. Gordon, "Illustrations from Pre-Nuzi Data on Biblical Archaeology," *The Biblical Archaeologist*, vol. 3, 1940, p. 5.

8. Changing the blessing between children was indeed quite common in the Ancient Near East during Biblical times. For example, a father named Tupkitilla of Nuzi sold one son's blessing to another for three sheep! C. H. Gordon, *Tyndale House Bulletin*, vol. 17, (1966), p. 71.

9. *Book of Jewish Knowledge.* p. 355.

10. A. Cohen, *Everyman's Talmud* (New York: Schocken Books, 1975), p. 171.

11. Ibid., p. 171.

12. How do we know that this group of children was both boys and girls? The Greek word used for *young children* in Mark 10:13 is *paidion*. (See William F. Arndt and R. Wilbur Gingrich, eds., *A Greek-English Lexicon of the New Testament and other Early Christian Literature* (Chicago: University of Chicago Press, 1957, p. 609). This was a general word used for little children of both sexes. There are specific Greek words that could have been used if the group was of all boys or all girls.

Chapter Three

1. K. M. Banham, "The Development of Affectionate Behavior in Infancy," *Journal of Genetic Psychology*, vol. 76:283–89 (1978).

2. Job 41:15–17; also see Brown, Driver, and Briggs, p. 621.

3. In Genesis 26:34 we are told that Esau was "forty years old" when he married. Since Jacob was his twin brother, it would naturally follow that he too was at least forty years old at the time of the blessing.

4. As we mentioned in Chapter Two, the blessing of Ephraim and Manasseh also had a unique spiritual message. When Jacob "crossed" his hands and blessed the younger with the older son's blessing, it was a picture of God's election.

5. Charles F. Pfeiffer, Howard F. Vos, John Rea, editors, *Wycliffe Bible Encyclopedia* (Chicago: Moody Press, 1975), p. 750.

6. Harvey Richard Schiffman, *Sensation and Perception: An Integrated Approach* (New York: John Wiley & Sons, 1982), p. 107.

7. Frank A. Geldard, "Body English," *Psychology Today*, December 1968, p. 44.

8. Dolores Krieger, "Therapeutic Touch: The Imprimatur of Nursing," *American Journal of Nursing*, May 1975, p. 784.

9. F. B. Dresslar, "The Psychology of Touch," *American Journal of Psychology*, vol. 6, 1984, p. 316.

10. *UCLA Monthly*, Alumni Association News, March–April 1981, p. 1.

11. Helen Colton, *The Gift of Touch* (New York: Seaview/ Putnam, 1983), p. 102.

12. Ibid., p. 49.

13. Arthur Janov, "For Control, Cults Must Ease the Most

Profound Pains," *Los Angeles Times,* Dec. 10, 1978, part 6, p. 3.

14. Marc H. Hollender, "The Wish to Be Held," *Archives of General Psychiatry,* vol. 22, 1970, p. 445.

15. Ibid., p. 446.

16. Ross Campbell, *How to Really Love Your Child* (Wheaton, Ill.: Victor Books, 1977), p. 73.

17. Alfred Edersheim, *The Life and Times of Jesus the Messiah, Part Two* (Grand Rapids: Wm. B. Eerdmans Publishing Co., 1972), p. 329.

Chapter Four
1. Gordon MacDonald, *Ordering Your Private World* (Nashville: Oliver Nelson Publishers, 1984).

2. Gary Smalley, *The Key to Your Child's Heart* (Waco, TX: Word Books, Inc., 1984). See the chapter on "Balancing Loving Support Through Contracts," pp. 77–107.

3. Jack Burton, "Goodbye . . . Be good to each other." Article in *USA Today,* August 19, 1985, p. 1.

Chapter Five
1. To "value" something in the Scriptures is captured in the word *honor* that we looked at in Chapter Two. See also, William F. Arndt and F. Wilbur Gingrich, editors, *A Greek-English Lexicon of the New Testament and other Early Christian Literature* (Chicago: The University of Chicago Press, 1957), p. 825.

2. Brown, Drive, and Briggs, *Hebrew Lexicon,* p. 139.

3. Ibid., p. 139.

4. That is why Psalm 95:6 translates the word *bless* as "to bow the knee" when it says, "Come let us worship the Lord and *bow before Him"* (literally *bless* Him).

5. J. D. Douglas, *New Bible Dictionary,* "Lion of Judah," (Grand Rapids: Wm. B. Eerdmans Publishing, 1971 edition), p. 742.

6. Some circles dispute over how Solomon, with all his many wives, could be a model for a godly marriage. One can see a commentary on the Song of Solomon for a fuller explanation, but in brief here are two reasons why we feel Solomon's story can still help any married couple today. First, Solomon did not begin to take foreign wives and concubines until later in life, after his visit by the Queen of Sheba. This book is dated by most scholars as being written early in his reign as king. Most importantly, *any person* including Solomon could leave their first love when they stop walking with God. During Solomon's later years when he took many wives, his fellowship

with God was certainly not where it was when he asked for the gift of wisdom.

7. S. Craig Glickman, *A Song for Lovers* (Downers Grove, IL: Inter-Varsity Press, 1974), p. 48.

Chapter Six

1. M. J. Cohen, *The Jewish Celebration Book* (Philadelphia: The Jewish Publication Society of America, 1946), p. 108.

2. Jay Stifler, *The Epistle to the Romans* (Chicago: Moody Press, 1983), p. 119.

3. While we do not recommend the book because of its secular bent and conclusions, William S. Appleton's *Fathers and Daughters* (New York: Berkley Books, 1984) has a number of chilling studies that have been done on the destruction that happens when a father has a poor relationship with his daughter.

4. We would like to extend our special thanks to Dr. Jeffry M. Trent, Associate Professor of Medicine, University of Arizona, for putting this example into "everyday English" for us.

Chapter Seven

1. For a helpful discussion on this point, see Charles Swindoll, *You and Your Child* (Nashville: Thomas Nelson Publishers, 1977), pp. 27–32.

2. Gary Smalley, *The Key to Your Child's Heart* (Word, 1984), Chapter Two, "Expressing Loving Support—The Most Important Aspect of Raising Children."

3. *The Key to Your Child's Heart*, Chapter Seven, "The Secret of a Close Knit Family."

4. Dewey Roussel, "Message of the White Dove," published in *Reader's Digest* September 1985, p. 29.

Chapter Eight

1. For an excellent discussion of our need today for a time of "Sabbath rest," see Gordon MacDonald's *Ordering Your Private World*, the chapter titled "Rest Beyond Leisure."

2. Quoted by Roger Hawley, "The Family Blessing: Implications for Counseling." Unpublished paper presented at the Texas Council of Family Relations Conference, 1983.

Chapter Nine

1. Quotation by Rev. Steven Lyon in "Loving Your Children God's Way," unpublished message given in Dallas, Texas, 1983.

2. An excellent book we would recommend that deals with

the impact family influences can have on both the creation and cure of substance abuse is entitled *Good News for the Chemically Dependent,* by Jeffrey VanVonderen (Thomas Nelson).

3. Richard A. McCormick, "Affective Disorders Among Pathological Gamblers Seeking Treatment," *American Journal of Psychiatry,* vol. 141, no. 2, p. 215.

Chapter Ten
1. *Hebrew Lexicon,* p. 866.

Chapter Eleven
1. *Hebrew Lexicon,* p. 174.

Chapter Twelve
1. Ken Medema, sound recording, *Through the Eyes of Love,* Word Records.

Chapter Thirteen
1. *Hebrew Lexicon,* p. 457.

2. Ibid., p. 866.

3. Arndt and Gingrich, *Greek-English Lexicon,* p. 317.

4. Gerald C. Davison and John M. Neale, *Abnormal Psychology* (New York: John Wiley & Sons, 1978), p. 135ff.

Appendix A
1. This suggestion is based on a creative church family evening in the excellent book by Marlene D. LeFever, *Creative Hospitality* (Wheaton, IL: Tyndale House Publishers, (1980), p. 26.

If you found this book to be helpful, or if you would like more information about the authors' national speaking schedule or other books and cassette tapes, please write to Today's Family, P.O. Box 22111, Phoenix, Ariz. 85028.